VEGAN

VEGAN

NUTRITIOUS, DELICIOUS PLANET-FRIENDLY MEALS

Project Editor Siobhán O'Connor
Project Designer Alison Shackleton
Editor Lucy Sienkowska
US Editor Alexandra Andrzejewski
US Consultant Renée Wilmeth
Jacket Designer Alison Donovan
Jackets Coordinator Jasmin Lennie
Production Editor David Almond
Production Controller Rebecca Parton
Managing Editor Dawn Henderson
Managing Art Editor Alison Donovan
Art Director Maxine Pedliham
Publishing Director Katie Cowan

First American Edition, 2023
Published in the United States by DK Publishing
1745 Broadway, 20th Floor, New York, NY 10019

Copyright © 2023 Dorling Kindersley Limited
DK, a Division of Penguin Random House LLC
23 24 25 26 27 10 9 8 7 6 5 4 3 2 1
001–333815–Mar/2023

A catalog record for this book is available from the Library of Congress.
ISBN 978-0-7440-7287-7

DK books are available at special discounts when purchased in bulk for sales
promotions, premiums, fund-raising, or educational use. For details, contact:
DK Publishing Special Markets, 1745 Broadway, 20th Floor, New York, NY 10019
SpecialSales@dk.com

Printed and bound in China

For the curious
www.dk.com

This book was made with Forest Stewardship Council™ certified paper—
one small step in DK's commitment to a sustainable future.
For more information go to **www.dk.com/our-green-pledge**

Contents

Introduction 6

Wake up **8**

Pack and go **48**

Big plates **90**

Sweet treats **144**

Conversion chart 188

Index 189

Acknowledgments 192

Plant-based living

A vegan diet is wholly plant-based and excludes all animal products. In addition to the obvious—no meat, seafood, eggs, or dairy products—honey, honeycomb, and gelatin are also off limits. There are also a few surprising places that animal products can lurk, so remember to check labels first if you are unsure.

What is a vegan diet?

A vegan diet is a varied and delicious option if you want to embrace a plant-based lifestyle. If you're already a vegetarian and ready to explore veganism, with only a few adjustments, you can enjoy a wide variety of ingredients and still maintain the nutrients you need for an active day. Best of all, a vegan diet doesn't mean you have to give up great-tasting food! Your diet will include the following:

LEGUMES Dried and canned lentils, chickpeas, cannellini or Great Northern beans, kidney beans, black-eyed peas, borlotti or cranberry beans, and split peas.

GRAINS AND GRAIN SUBSTITUTES/PSEUDO-GRAINS Amaranth, barley, buckwheat, freekeh, oats, rice, farro, millet, polenta, quinoa, and wheat-based products such as a variety of flours, couscous, and bulgur wheat.

NUTS AND SEEDS Almonds, cashews, peanuts, pecans, pistachios, macadamias, walnuts, sunflower seeds, pumpkin seeds, flaxseeds, chia seeds, and sesame seeds, as well as unhulled and hulled tahini.

SOY PRODUCTS Tofu, tempeh, and other soy products, including miso paste and vegan "cheeses."

ALTERNATIVE DAIRY PRODUCTS There are a wide range of dairy-like products now available, including soy milk, rice milk, almond milk, coconut milk, and oat milk, and plant-based yogurts such as coconut yogurt. You can also find many vegan "cheeses."

SEA VEGETABLES Kelps, seaweeds such as dulse, nori, kombu, and wakame, as well as spirulina.

HERBS AND SPICES Dried spices including cardamom, cinnamon, cloves, coriander, cumin, fennel seeds, garam masala, garlic powder, ginger, mustard seeds and powder, nutmeg, onion powder, paprika, and turmeric. Fresh herbs such as basil, cilantro, dill, parsley, mint, oregano, rosemary, and thyme.

CONDIMENTS Including soy sauce, tamari, miso, vinegars, mustards, and nutritional yeast flakes.

Your nutritional needs

When planning vegan meals, especially when just starting out, the most frequently asked questions are about how to incorporate all the necessary nutrients into your diet. To help avoid potential deficiencies, here are the most common nutrients that cause concern, together with suggestions for vegan sources to meet your dietary needs:

CALCIUM In place of dairy products, use nuts, seeds, leafy green vegetables, legumes, and soy products, especially those that are fortified with calcium.

IODINE Include sea vegetables such as nori, kombu, or wakame, and small amounts of iodized salt. Check with your doctor before taking supplements if you have a thyroid disorder.

IRON Eat nuts, lentils, oats, dried fruit, dark leafy green vegetables, and soy products. Eating these in tandem with fresh foods rich in vitamin C aids the body in better absorbing the iron.

VITAMIN C Include tomatoes, red peppers, broccoli, citrus fruits, and berries in your diet.

OMEGA-3 FATTY ACIDS Include flaxseeds, chia seeds, pumpkin seeds, seaweed, spirulina, and walnuts.

PROTEIN Eat legumes, whole grains, quinoa, nuts, seeds, and soy products, especially tofu and tempeh.

VITAMIN B12 As this vitamin is found naturally only in meat, some fish, dairy, and eggs, make sure to incorporate foods fortified with vitamin B12, such as some cereals, plant-based milks, and soy products. A supplement can be taken as well.

ZINC Add whole grains, nuts, pumpkin seeds, wheatgerm, and soy products, especially tofu and tempeh.

Your day on a plate

ACTIVE PERSON If you fall into this category, especially if you are female and premenopausal, it's vital you eat as varied a diet as possible. If not, you risk an inadequate dietary intake for optimum health. For the active vegan, incorporate energy-dense foods such as nuts, tofu, tempeh, and other quality protein at every meal. Because vegetable proteins don't include all the necessary amino acids, it's important to combine a variety of proteins throughout the day. Plant-based proteins are not as easily digested as meat-derived ones, so it's advised that you consume 10 percent more per day. If you are vegan and super-active, it is especially important to target iron-rich foods and monitor your iron stores. To ensure sufficient calcium intake, look for calcium-rich vegan foods such as almonds and leafy greens.

MODERATELY ACTIVE PERSON The nutritional requirements of a moderately active person are very similar to that of an active person. The main difference between the two is your overall calorie requirements will be less. Keep an eye on your carbohydrate consumption and be careful not to rely too heavily on carbs to bulk up your diet. As with a vegan diet in general, eating widely from all plant-based foods is key to ensuring you capture vital nutrients and are not missing out on certain nutritional requirements that can be harder to meet in a vegan diet. Be aware, too, that many vegan foods are not necessarily healthy. In fact, manufactured vegan substitutes can be laden with not-so-nutritious bulking agents that add unnecessarily to your calorie quota. Just because a sweet treat is vegan doesn't afford it health-food status!

WAKE UP

Sweet or savory, energy-boosting or indulgent, there are breakfasts here for every day of the week, from satisfying mueslis to irresistible pancakes and waffles.

Turmeric tofu scramble

PREP + COOK TIME **15 MINUTES** | SERVES **2**

Tofu is an excellent source of calcium, and a 3.5 oz (100g) serving of tofu will also provide you with 8g of protein, making this dish an energy-giving start to the day. It also works well for a weekend brunch or even a casual lunch with family or friends.

8.5 oz (250g) firm tofu

2 tsp nutritional yeast flakes (optional; see tips)

1/2 tsp ground turmeric

1/2 tsp cumin seeds

1/4 tsp smoked paprika

2 tbsp olive oil

4 green onions, thinly sliced

1 garlic clove, crushed

1 tbsp coarsely chopped flat-leaf parsley

1 tbsp lemon juice

4 bagels, split, toasted

1/3 cup (85g) hummus (see tips)

2 tomatoes (300g), sliced

1/2 cup (50g) baby spinach leaves

1/2 cup (25g) microgreens or other pea shoots

salt and freshly ground black pepper

1 Pat the tofu dry with paper towels to remove excess moisture. Using your hands, crumble the tofu into a small bowl. Set aside.

2 Combine the nutritional yeast flakes (if using), turmeric, cumin seeds, smoked paprika, and 1 tablespoon water in a small bowl; season with salt and pepper to taste.

3 Heat the olive oil in a medium skillet over medium-high heat; cook the green onions and garlic for 1 minute or until softened. Add the crumbled tofu; cook, stirring, for 4 minutes or until the tofu starts to brown a little. Add the spice mixture; cook, stirring, for 1 minute or until the tofu is completely coated in the spices. Stir in the parsley and lemon juice until combined. Season with salt and pepper.

4 Spread the toasted bagel halves with the hummus; top with the tomato, scrambled tofu, spinach leaves, and pea shoots. Sandwich with the top halves of the bagels to serve.

TIPS

- As a seasoning, nutritional yeast flakes provide a cheesy, umami taste. Look for a brand that is fortified with B12, an essential vitamin found naturally in meat, fish, dairy, and eggs, and therefore needs to be supplemented in a vegan diet.
- To add a smoky flavor to the scrambled tofu, simply use smoked tofu. You can also add any spice you'd like to the hummus, including harissa, chipotle powder, taco seasoning, or smoked paprika.
- Top with other greens such as arugula and watercress, if preferred.

Chocolate pancakes with maple banana

PREP + COOK TIME **20 MINUTES + STANDING** | SERVES **2**

Some flavor pairings are considered classics for a reason: they are very hard to resist. Chocolate and banana definitely fall into this category. The treat factor is increased by caramelizing the bananas in a little maple syrup first, before using them to top the pancakes.

2 tbsp vegetable oil

2 bananas (260g)

2 tbsp pure maple syrup, plus extra to serve

1/2 cup (140g) coconut yogurt (use Homemade Coconut Yogurt on page 21 or purchase premade)

3/4 cup (100g) fresh cherries

pancake batter

1 1/3 cups (185g) all-purpose flour

2 tbsp Dutch-process cocoa powder

2 tsp baking powder

2 tsp baking soda

1/2 tsp salt

1/2 tsp ground cinnamon

3/4 cup (180ml) almond milk

2 tsp apple cider vinegar

1/3 cup (80ml) pure maple syrup

1 Make the pancake batter. Sift the flour, cocoa powder, baking powder, baking soda, salt, and cinnamon into a medium bowl. Whisk together the almond milk, apple cider vinegar, and maple syrup in a small bowl. Make a well in the center of the flour mixture. Gradually pour in the almond milk mixture, whisking continuously, until a smooth batter forms. Allow to stand for 5 minutes.

2 Heat a large nonstick skillet over medium heat; brush with a little of the vegetable oil. Working in batches, pour the pancake batter into the pan, using about 1/4 cup (60ml) batter for each pancake. Cook for 2 minutes or until bubbles appear on the surface. Turn the pancakes; cook for a further 1 minute on the other side or until lightly browned. Remove from the pan; cover to keep warm. Repeat with the remaining oil and batter to make 8 pancakes in total. Reserve the pan.

3 Slice the bananas on a sharp angle. Place the reserved pan over medium-high heat. Add the maple syrup and bananas to the hot pan; cook for 2 minutes or until caramelized; turn and cook for a further 30 seconds.

4 Serve the pancakes topped with the coconut yogurt, caramelized bananas, cherries, and an extra drizzle of maple syrup.

TIPS

- Dutch-process cocoa powder is treated with an alkalizing ingredient to neutralize cocoa's naturally acidic taste, making it smoother and more mellow.
- Use your favorite berries instead of cherries.
- The pancakes can be frozen for up to 1 month; simply reheat from frozen when needed.

Spiced pecan French toast

PREP + COOK TIME **25 MINUTES** | SERVES **4**

The trick to cooking this toast perfectly is to keep an eye on the heat to ensure the nuts don't scorch. The result is crisp-coated, spice-infused heaven, and the sweet acidity of the fresh berries provides the ideal counterbalance to the rich flavors and textures.

1½ cups (375ml) canned coconut milk

2 tsp vanilla extract

½ cup (125ml) pure maple syrup, divided

⅓ cup (35g) hazelnut meal

1 tbsp nutritional yeast flakes (see tips)

¼ tsp ground cinnamon

⅛ tsp ground allspice

⅛ tsp ground nutmeg

1 cup (120g) pecans, finely chopped

8 thick slices of multigrain sourdough bread

3 tbsp (40g) vegan margarine spread, divided

2 cups (250g) mixed berries such as strawberries, blueberries, and raspberries

2 tsp vegan powdered sugar

unsprayed edible flowers (optional)

1 Whisk together the coconut milk, vanilla, 2 tablespoons of the maple syrup, hazelnut meal, nutritional yeast flakes, cinnamon, allspice, and nutmeg in a shallow dish. Put the pecans on a plate, spreading in an even layer. Soak the bread in the coconut milk mixture, a slice at a time, for 1 minute on each side. Press onto the pecans.

2 Heat half of the margarine in a large skillet over medium-low heat. Cook the bread in batches for 2 minutes on each side or until golden, adding the remaining margarine halfway through cooking.

3 Divide the French toast among 4 serving plates; top with the berries and remaining syrup. Dust with the powdered sugar. Serve topped with edible flowers, if you'd like.

TIPS

- Use almond meal instead of hazelnut meal, if you'd like, and olive oil instead of vegan margarine spread.
- Nutritional yeast is deactivated yeast, having been heat-treated so that it cannot ferment. A complete protein, it contains 18 amino acids, including the nine that are essential for good health.
- Powdered sugar can be produced with animal products used in the refining process. Look for vegan powdered sugar to ensure it's animal-product free.

Fig and orange chia pudding

PREP + COOK TIME **15 MINUTES + STANDING + REFRIGERATION** | SERVES **4**

Figs and chia seeds are sources of dietary fiber and protein, which make you feel full. They are also, along with almonds, nondairy sources of calcium. Turkish figs are traditionally sun-dried, making them meatier and more aromatic than other dried figs.

You will need to start this recipe at least 2 hours ahead

5 dried Turkish figs (80g)

2 cups (500ml) almond milk

1 tsp vanilla extract

1 tbsp pure maple syrup

1 tsp finely grated orange zest, plus extra strips of zest to decorate (optional; see tips)

$^{1}/_{2}$ cup (80g) white chia seeds, plus extra to decorate (optional)

1 cup (280g) coconut yogurt (use Homemade Coconut Yogurt on page 21 or purchase premade)

1 cup (150g) blueberries, divided

1 cup (150g) blackberries

2 small fresh figs (100g), cut into wedges

$^{1}/_{2}$ cup (75g) cherries

$^{1}/_{4}$ cup unsprayed edible flowers (optional)

1 Remove the stems and put the dried figs in a small bowl with 1 cup (250ml) water; allow to stand for at least 2 hours. Drain the figs, discarding the liquid.

2 Put the drained figs in a high-powered blender with the almond milk, vanilla extract, maple syrup, and orange zest; blend until smooth. Transfer the mixture to a medium bowl; whisk in the chia seeds until evenly combined.

3 Pour the mixture into four $^{3}/_{4}$-cup (180ml) glasses, bowls, or dishes. Cover, then refrigerate for at least 2 hours or overnight.

4 Blend the yogurt and half of the blueberries until smooth; spoon the yogurt mixture over the fig mixture, dividing evenly among the glasses.

5 Serve the puddings topped with the blackberries, remaining blueberries, fresh figs, and cherries. Sprinkle with extra strips of orange zest, extra chia seeds, and edible flowers, if you'd like.

TIPS

• These puddings are best made the night before serving. They will keep for up to 3 days in the fridge.

• To make orange zest to decorate, use a zester to remove the zest from half an orange. (Or thinly peel the zest from the orange using a vegetable peeler; remove any white pith, then cut the zest into long, thin strips.)

• For a summery dessert, decorate the puddings with heart-shaped vegan chocolates.

Nut and seed butter

PREP + COOK TIME **30 MINUTES** | MAKES **1¹/₂ CUPS**

This delicious nondairy butter alternative is suitable not only for vegans, but also for those who are lactose-intolerant. The butter is very lightly sweetened but can still be used as a spread for savory sandwiches. Simply omit the maple syrup, if you'd like.

1 cup (160g) blanched almonds, roasted

¹/₂ cup (70g) roasted unsalted peanuts

¹/₂ cup (75g) sunflower seeds

¹/₄ cup (40g) flaxseeds

¹/₄ cup (60ml) light-flavored extra virgin olive oil

1 tbsp pure maple syrup

¹/₂ tsp sea salt flakes

1 In the bowl of a food processor, process all of the ingredients, scraping the side of the bowl regularly, until the mixture is smooth. Alternatively, use a high-powered blender for a faster and smoother result. (This step may take up to 25 minutes depending on the processing power of your processor or blender. Powerful commercial processors and blenders will take around 10 minutes, while ordinary blenders/processors can take up to 25 minutes before the mixture becomes smooth.)

2 Spoon the nut and seed butter into a jar with a tight-fitting lid; refrigerate. It will keep, refrigerated in an airtight container, for up to 3 weeks. Stir before using, as the oil will settle on the top.

3 Spread the nut and seed butter on your favorite toast or crispbread, then top with fruit such as sliced melon, kiwi, mandarin orange segments, thinly sliced apple, sliced strawberries, sliced avocado with sesame seeds or edible flowers, sliced banana, or blueberries.

TIPS

• If you'd like, swap the almonds and peanuts for cashews and macadamias; omit the flaxseeds, and stir in 2 tablespoons poppy seeds at the end.

• For a chocolaty breakfast spread, add 1¹/₂ tablespoons Dutch-process cocoa powder and an extra 1 tablespoon maple syrup to the ingredients.

• For crunchy nut butter, reserve ¹/₂ cup (about 75g) of the nuts, and pulse through at the end of blending.

Homemade coconut yogurt

PREP + COOK TIME 15 MINUTES + STERILIZATION + STANDING + REFRIGERATION | MAKES 4³/₄ CUPS (ABOUT 1.3KG)

Best enjoyed for breakfast or as a dessert topped with fresh or poached fruit, this coconut milk yogurt is not suitable for cooking. Remember that you will need to start the recipe 2 days ahead to allow time for fermentation. Also, the yogurt mixture is poured into sterilized jars to set; see the instructions for sterilizing jars below. Don't skip this step—it's important!

You will need to start this recipe 2 days ahead

¹/₄ cup (30g) tapioca flour (see tips)

3¹/₃ cups (800ml) canned coconut milk, divided (see tips)

1²/₃ cups (400ml) canned coconut cream (see tips)

3 vegan probiotic yogurt starter capsules (see tips)

1 tbsp pure maple syrup

fresh fruit and unsprayed edible flowers, to serve

1 Sterilize the jars (see below).

2 Whisk the tapioca flour and ¹/₄ cup (60ml) of the coconut milk in a small bowl until smooth and combined.

3 Pour the tapioca mixture into a medium saucepan; whisk in the remaining coconut milk and the coconut cream until combined. Stir the mixture over low heat for 10 minutes or until it boils and thickens. Remove the pan from the heat. Place a cooking thermometer in the pan, then allow to stand until the mixture cools to 109°F (43°C). Once cooled, open the probiotic capsules; add the powder inside, along with the maple syrup, to the yogurt mixture, and stir to combine.

4 Transfer the mixture to the warm sterilized jars; seal immediately. Allow to stand in a warm place for 12 hours or until cultured (the mixture will taste slightly sour) and slightly thickened. Refrigerate for 24 hours or until the coconut yogurt thickens further. The coconut yogurt will keep refrigerated for up to 2 weeks.

5 Serve topped with kiwi, figs, blueberries, raspberries, and edible flowers, or any combination of seasonal fruits you'd like.

sterilizing jars Make sure your glass storage jars have no chips or cracks and any lids provide an airtight seal. Hygiene is important, so ensure your hands are clean and use clean kitchen towels when holding or moving the jars. Run the jars and lids through the hot rinse cycle in a dishwasher, or wash them in hot soapy water; rinse well. Stand the clean jars, top-side up, on a tray in a cold oven; heat to 250°F (120°C), then leave the jars in the oven for 30 minutes.

TIPS

- Tapioca flour, also known as tapioca starch, is gluten-free and available from large supermarkets, health food shops, and specialty and Asian grocers, as well as online.
- Buy coconut milk and coconut cream without additives, preservatives, and stabilizers; otherwise the set of the yogurt may be affected.
- Probiotic capsules are readily available from pharmacies and health food shops.
- You can keep this yogurt on hand in the refrigerator to use as a fresh topping for muesli, porridge, or pancakes, if you'd like.

Bircher muesli

While regular muesli is cooked or toasted in the oven before eating, Bircher muesli is made of oats that have been soaked overnight in nut milk or fruit juice. It's perfect for a raw food diet and considered the original version of overnight oats.

Super seed Bircher

PREP TIME **15 MINUTES + REFRIGERATION** | SERVES **4**

Crumble $1/2$ cup (25g) coconut flakes into a medium bowl. Stir in $1/3$ cup (55g) sunflower seeds, $1/3$ cup (55g) pumpkin seeds, $1/4$ cup (40g) white chia seeds, $1/4$ cup (25g) flaxseed meal, and 1¼ cups (310ml) almond milk. Cover, then refrigerate for at least 1 hour or overnight. Cut 2 green apples (300g) into matchsticks, and thickly slice 1$1/2$ cups (200g) strawberries. Divide the seed mixture among 4 serving bowls; top with the apple and strawberries. Drizzle with coconut nectar syrup or pure maple syrup to serve.

Make-and-go Bircher

PREP TIME **10 MINUTES** | SERVES **2**

Cut 1 large ripe banana (230g) in half. Place each half in a 2-cup (500ml) glass jar; mash with a fork. Cut 1 large red dessert apple (200g) with the skin on into matchsticks; divide evenly between the jars. Add $1/2$ cup (50g) rolled oats and a pinch of ground cinnamon. Top each jar with 1 tablespoon pumpkin seeds and 2 tablespoons blueberries. Stir $3/4$ cup (185ml) almond and coconut milk into each jar. Seal and go.

Pomegranate and pear Bircher

PREP TIME **15 MINUTES + REFRIGERATION** | SERVES **6**

Combine 2 cups (500ml) almond milk and 1 cup (250ml) pomegranate juice in a medium bowl. Add 1 cup (95g) rolled oats, $1/2$ cup (40g) quinoa flakes, and 2 tablespoons white chia seeds; stir to combine. Grate 1 large pear (330g); add to the oat mixture. Stir to combine. Cover, then refrigerate for 3 hours or overnight. Divide the oats among 6 serving bowls; drizzle with pure maple syrup. Top each serving with 1 tablespoon pomegranate seeds, 2 slices of pear, and a little grated orange zest.

Coconut tropical Bircher

PREP TIME **15 MINUTES** | SERVES **4**

Combine 3 cups (240g) quinoa flakes, 1 cup (250ml) canned coconut milk, 1 cup (250ml) coconut water, and 1 cup (250ml) cloudy apple juice in a medium bowl. Divide the mixture evenly among 4 serving bowls. Cut 1 small dragon fruit (250g) and 1 small mango (300g) into slices; divide the fruit evenly among the bowls. Serve the Bircher topped with the pulp of 1 passion fruit and $1/4$ cup (15g) coconut flakes.

TIP

Pomegranate seeds (arils) are sold in small containers in the fresh food section.

Crunch bowl with berry coconut yogurt

PREP + COOK TIME **40 MINUTES** | SERVES **6**

Seeds are a good source of protein, fiber, and minerals, and pumpkin seeds contain a surprising amount of iron for their size. Inca berries—also known as cape gooseberries or golden berries—are native to South America and have a wonderful tangy flavor.

1 cup (160g) raw Brazil nuts

½ cup (80g) raw almonds

⅓ cup (65g) raw pumpkin seeds

⅓ cup (50g) raw sunflower seeds

⅔ cup (30g) unsweetened coconut flakes

¼ cup (35g) cacao nibs

⅔ cup (110g) Inca golden berries

3 cups (840g) berry coconut yogurt

fresh fruit and unsprayed edible flowers, to serve (see tips)

1 Preheat the oven to 350°F (180°C). Line a baking sheet with parchment paper. Spread the Brazil nuts and almonds in an even layer on the baking sheet; roast for 10 minutes or until lightly browned and fragrant. Coarsely chop the Brazil nuts and almonds; place in a large bowl.

2 Roast the seeds on the baking sheet for 8 minutes or until lightly browned; add to the bowl. Roast the coconut on the baking sheet for 4 minutes or until lightly browned and fragrant. Add to the bowl, along with the cacao nibs and Inca golden berries; stir to mix evenly.

3 Spoon the crunch bowl mixture into 6 serving bowls, followed by the yogurt. Serve the crunch bowl topped with dragon fruit, honeydew melon, figs, kiwi, cherries, blueberries, strawberries, pomegranate seeds, and raspberries, along with edible flowers (as in the photograph).

TIPS

- Any combination of nuts and seeds can be used in this recipe, or choose your favorite flavor of coconut yogurt instead of berry, if you'd like.
- Dried Inca golden berries (also known as Cape gooseberries or dried ground cherries) are high in vitamins C, B, and A, and are available at some supermarkets, health food shops, and online.
- Use any combination of seasonal fruits you'd like, adjusting the makeup according to the time of year.
- Make the most of this versatile crunch bowl mix. Serve with oatmeal or sprinkle on top of yogurt or fruit, scattered with unsprayed edible flowers and vegan chocolate, if you'd like. It also doubles as a trail mix for an energy-rich snack on the go.

Cherry tomato and "mozzarella" bruschetta

PREP + COOK TIME **40 MINUTES + SOAKING + COOLING + REFRIGERATION** | SERVES **4**

If you have it, day-old bread is ideal for bruschetta. The bread will be revived by the gorgeous tomato juices and still retain its texture. To turn this into lunch or a light supper, serve with a side salad topped with sunflower seeds.

You will need to start the vegan mozzarella recipe at least 4 hours ahead

1 lb (400g) vine tomato medley mix

8 oz (225g) cherry vine tomatoes

1 tbsp fresh rosemary or oregano leaves

4 garlic cloves, bruised, halved

2 tbsp olive oil

2 tbsp balsamic drizzle (see tips)

8 thick slices of soy and flaxseed sourdough bread

$^2/_3$ cup (150g) vegan mozzarella (see right or use store-bought)

salt and freshly ground black pepper

arugula and walnut pesto

5 cups (100g) arugula, coarsely chopped

$^1/_2$ cup (80g) toasted walnuts, coarsely chopped

2 tbsp nutritional yeast flakes

$^1/_2$ cup (125ml) olive oil

TIPS

• For the balsamic drizzle, use balsamic glaze, white balsamic, or traditional aged balsamic vinegar.
• You can buy premade mozzarella-style vegan cheese instead of making your own, or swap for vegan cream cheese instead (as pictured here).
• Use vegan mozzarella as a cheese substitute on pizzas or in toasted sandwiches and bakes. It keeps in a covered container in the fridge for up to 1 week.

1 Make the arugula and walnut pesto. Process the ingredients in a small food processor until almost smooth. Transfer to a small bowl; season with salt and pepper to taste.

2 When ready to make the bruschetta, preheat the oven to 350°F (180°C).

3 Arrange the tomatoes, rosemary, and garlic on a medium baking sheet. Drizzle with the olive oil and balsamic drizzle; season well with salt and pepper. Roast for 20 minutes. Allow to cool for 5 minutes. Lightly crush the tomatoes; reserve the cooking juices on the tray.

4 Meanwhile, toast the sourdough slices.

5 Top each toast with some of the mozzarella, followed by the tomato mixture. Drizzle with the reserved cooking juices from the tray and the arugula and walnut pesto.

vegan mozzarella Put $^1/_2$ cup (75g) raw cashews in a small bowl; cover with 3 cups (750ml) cold water. Allow to stand, covered, for 4 hours or overnight. Drain the cashews, then rinse under cold water; drain well. Put in a high-powered blender with $^1/_2$ cup (70g) macadamias, $^2/_3$ cup (100g) arrowroot powder, $^1/_4$ cup (60ml) olive oil, $^1/_4$ cup (25g) nutritional yeast flakes, 2 teaspoons sea salt flakes, and 2 tablespoons lemon juice. Blend until smooth. Pour the mixture into a medium saucepan. Cook, stirring, over medium heat for 9 minutes or until the mixture becomes very thick and stretchy like melted cheese. Pour the mixture into a 3-cup (750ml) container; allow to cool. Cover with the lid; refrigerate until needed. The mozzarella, which is spreadable, will keep in an airtight container in the fridge for up to 1 week.

Buckini and berry granola clusters

PREP + COOK TIME **25 MINUTES + COOLING** | MAKES **ABOUT 5 CUPS (550G)**

This toasted granola is streets ahead of shop-bought versions. Serve the clusters with nut,
oat, or soy milk and vegan coconut yogurt (see Homemade Coconut Yogurt on page 21),
or alternatively sprinkle over stone fruit or berries as a crunchy topping.

1 cup (110g) rolled oats

1 tsp ground allspice

1/2 tsp ground cardamom

1/2 tsp sea salt flakes

2 tbsp rice malt syrup (see tips)

1 tbsp coconut oil, melted

1 cup (180g) activated buckinis (see tips)

1 cup (30g) puffed quinoa

1 cup (30g) puffed buckwheat

1/4 cup (30g) goji berries

1/4 cup (35g) dried cranberries

1/4 cup (40g) chia seeds

3/4 cup (75g) freeze-dried pomegranate seeds

1 Preheat the oven to 350°F (180°C).

2 Spread the oats in an even layer on a large shallow-sided baking sheet.
Sprinkle with the spices and salt, then drizzle with the rice malt syrup
and coconut oil; toss to coat. Bake for 10 minutes or until the mixture is
sticky and golden, stirring once during the cooking time. Allow to cool,
then break into clusters. Use a spatula to scrape the mixture from the
tray, as it will be caramelized.

3 Put the remaining ingredients in a large bowl with the oat clusters;
toss to combine. Store in a glass jar with a tight-fitting lid or a similar
airtight container. The granola will keep at room temperature for up to
2 months.

TIPS

• If you can't find rice malt syrup, you can substitute
barley malt syrup or agave syrup.

• Buckinis, also known as activated buckwheat,
are crunchy groats—a great addition to granola. You
can replace with puffed quinoa or buckwheat with
puffed rice, if you'd like.

• Any dried fruit works well here. Try to buy
sulphate-free dried fruit that has no added sugar.
Freeze-dried pomegranate seeds are available from
some supermarkets and health food shops.

• To make your own granola bars, heat some rice
malt syrup until bubbling and beginning to
caramelize; stir in the granola. Press into a
rectangular or square shallow cake tin lined with
baking parchment. Allow to cool, then cut into bars.

Baked oatmeal with stone fruit

PREP + COOK TIME **55 MINUTES** | SERVES **6**

Although baked oatmeal takes longer to cook than the usual stove-top method, it is still convenient because it cooks without stirring or tending and rewards you with a delicious creaminess. Serve with a dollop of Homemade Coconut Yogurt on page 21, if you'd like.

$1^{1}/_{2}$ cups (135g) rolled oats

$1/_2$ cup (40g) dried coconut flakes

$1/_2$ tsp ground cinnamon

$1/_2$ tsp ground ginger

pinch of sea salt

$1/_4$ cup (90g) pure maple syrup

1 tsp vanilla extract

3 cups (750ml) rice milk

2 rhubarb stems (125g), trimmed, cut into $1^{1}/_{2}$ in (4cm) lengths

3 plums (350g), halved

2 nectarines or peaches (340g), cut into thick wedges

2 tbsp coconut sugar

unsprayed edible flowers, to serve (optional)

1 Preheat the oven to 350°F (180°C). Grease a 6-quart (5.5-liter) ovenproof dish.

2 In the dish, combine the rolled oats, coconut, cinnamon, ginger, sea salt, maple syrup, and vanilla extract; stir in the rice milk.

3 Bake for 40 minutes or until the oats are tender and creamy.

4 Meanwhile, put the rhubarb and stone fruit in a small baking dish. Sprinkle with the coconut sugar and $1/_3$ cup (80ml) water. Bake with the oatmeal, on a separate shelf, for the last 20 minutes of the oatmeal cooking time.

5 Serve the oatmeal topped with the baked fruit and its syrup and edible flowers, if you'd like.

TIPS

- You can use soy, almond, or coconut milk in place of the rice milk, if you'd like.
- In winter, try roasted pears instead of nectarines or peaches. Firm pears may take a little longer to cook, so don't forget to factor this in.

Chickpea pancakes with spicy pinto beans

PREP + COOK TIME **30 MINUTES** | SERVES **4**

Chickpea flour has a wonderful nutty taste and a naturally higher protein content than wheat-based flours; it is also gluten-free. The trick when adding the water to the flour for the pancake batter is to ensure that the water is cool from the tap, not hot.

1 cup (260g) hummus

2 canned chipotle chilies in adobo sauce

2 cups (300g) chickpea flour (besan or gram flour)

1 tsp baking powder

1 tsp garlic powder

¼ cup (60ml) olive oil, divided

2½ cups (80g) kale leaves, thinly sliced

2 (15 oz/425g) cans pinto beans

1 tbsp taco seasoning or chili powder

2 avocados (500g)

4 radishes (140g), trimmed

½ cup (15g) loosely packed cilantro

salt and freshly ground black pepper

1 lime, cut into wedges

1 Blend or process the hummus and chipotle chillies until combined. Set aside until needed.

2 Whisk together the chickpea flour, baking powder, and garlic powder in a medium bowl until well combined. Make a well in the center. Add 2 cups (500ml) water; whisk until the mixture forms a batter. Season with salt and pepper to taste.

3 Heat 1 tablespoon of the olive oil in a large nonstick skillet over medium heat; cook the kale, stirring, for 2 minutes or until wilted. Remove from the pan; cover to keep warm.

4 Heat another 2 teaspoons of the olive oil in the same pan. Add a quarter of the pancake mixture; cook over medium-high heat for 2 minutes on each side or until light golden. Transfer to a plate; cover to keep warm. Repeat with the remaining olive oil and pancake batter to make 4 pancakes in total.

5 Meanwhile, stir the beans and spice mix in a small saucepan over low heat until hot. Thinly slice the avocados and radishes to have ready with the other pancake toppings.

6 Serve the pancakes topped with the hummus mixture, beans, avocado, wilted kale, radishes, cilantro, and lime wedges.

TIPS

- The pancakes are best served the same day.
- You can use spinach or Swiss chard in place of the kale.
- The beans can be heated in the microwave.

Pea and edamame toast with avocado and umeboshi

PREP + COOK TIME **25 MINUTES** | MAKES **4**

Umeboshi, or Japanese pickled plums, have an intense salty–sour flavor and are used as
a condiment in Japanese cuisine. They also have a long history of use as a traditional remedy,
believed to reduce fatigue, stimulate digestion, and eliminate toxins.

1 cup (100g) frozen edamame

1 cup (120g) frozen green peas

½ cup (10g) loosely packed mint leaves

1 tbsp lemon juice

4 tbsp olive oil, divided

4 slices of sourdough bread

1 tbsp umeboshi paste (see tips)

1 small avocado (200g), sliced

2 watermelon radishes (70g), trimmed, thinly sliced

1 tbsp microgreens

salt and freshly ground black pepper

1 Add the edamame to a medium saucepan of boiling water; cook for
2 minutes. Add the frozen peas; cook for a further 2 minutes or until
tender. Drain; rinse under cold water to refresh and stop the cooking
process. Shell the edamame; discard the pods.

2 Process the edamame, peas, and mint until combined but still chunky.
Add the lemon juice and a small drizzle of olive oil. With the motor
operating, gradually add 2 tablespoons olive oil in a thin stream until
the mixture is a spreadable consistency. Transfer to a small bowl; season
with salt and pepper to taste.

3 Brush each slice of bread with a little of the remaining olive oil. Toast
the bread on a heated grill plate or in a ridged cast-iron grill pan over
high heat until browned on both sides.

4 Spread the sourdough toast with the umeboshi paste and pea mixture.
Top with the avocado, radishes, and microgreens. Season with salt and
pepper to taste. Drizzle with a little more olive oil, if you'd like.

TIPS

• Umeboshi paste, made from fermented
Japanese ume plums, is available from
apanese grocers and some health food stores.

• The pea mixture can be made several hours
ahead. Prepare from step 3 just before serving.

Peanut butter and maple syrup crunch

PREP + COOK TIME 1 HOUR + COOLING | MAKES 4 CUPS (ABOUT 600G)

Flaxseeds (also known as golden linseeds) are a rich source of heart-healthy omega-3 fatty acids and may help in the prevention of some cancers. Serve the crunch topped with coconut yogurt, apple, raspberries, nut, or soy milk, then drizzled with extra maple syrup.

$^1/_3$ cup (95g) smooth natural peanut butter

$^1/_4$ cup (50g) coconut oil

$^1/_4$ cup (90g) pure maple syrup

1 tsp vanilla extract

$1^1/_2$ cups (135g) rolled oats

$1^1/_2$ cups (150g) rolled barley

$^1/_4$ cup (50g) amaranth grain (see tips)

$^1/_3$ cup (65g) pumpkin seeds

2 tbsp flaxseeds

$^1/_3$ cup (45g) chopped roasted salted peanuts

1 Preheat the oven to 325°F (160°C). Line 2 baking sheets with parchment paper.

2 Stir together the peanut butter, coconut oil, maple syrup, and vanilla in a small saucepan over low heat until melted and smooth.

3 Combine the rolled oats, rolled barley, and amaranth in a large bowl. Pour in the peanut butter mixture; stir until combined. Spread on the lined trays in an even layer.

4 Bake for 20 minutes, stirring once. Stir in the pumpkin seeds and flaxseeds; bake for a further 30 minutes, stirring every 10 minutes, or until golden. Stir in the peanuts; allow to cool on the trays. Store in an airtight container until needed.

TIPS

- An ancient grain, amaranth is a pseudocereal similar to quinoa and buckwheat. Gluten-free and a good source of fiber and essential vitamins and minerals, the seeds can be toasted, baked, ground into flour, or used in a porridge, but must always be cooked before eating.
- You can replace the rolled barley with extra rolled oats. Amaranth can be replaced with chia seeds.
- The crunch will keep in an airtight glass jar or container for up to 1 month.

Spinach and tomato "omelet"

PREP + COOK TIME **20 MINUTES** | MAKES **2**

Making your own nut-based marinated vegan feta is easy, and it's a great stand-by to have
in the fridge. Simply follow the recipe below so that you have it on hand when you need it.
The longer you allow the feta to marinate, the stronger the flavors will be.

**You will need to start the feta at least
1 day ahead, if making**

10 oz (300g) silken tofu

2 tbsp olive oil, divided

1/3 cup (80ml) soy milk

1/3 cup (50g) chickpea flour (besan or gram flour)

2 tbsp nutritional yeast flakes

1/2 tsp sea salt flakes

1/4 tsp ground turmeric

spinach filling

4 cups (120g) fresh spinach leaves

1 shallot, thinly sliced

8 oz (225g) heirloom cherry tomatoes,
sliced or halved

1 tbsp red wine vinegar

2 tbsp olive oil

2oz (60g) drained marinated vegan feta (see tip)

TIP

There are various feta-style vegan cheeses
available at the grocery store if you don't want to
make your own. You could also use other styles of
vegan cheese or crumbled tofu or tempeh.

1   To make the omelet mixture, pat the tofu dry with paper towels.
Blend the tofu with 1 tablespoon of the olive oil and the remaining
ingredients in a blender until smooth.

2   Heat an 8-inch (22cm) nonstick skillet over high heat. Add 2 teaspoons
of the olive oil; reduce the heat to medium-high. Add half of the tofu
mixture; swirl or spread the mixture until the bottom of the pan is
covered. Cook for 3 minutes or until small bubbles appear on the surface.
Slide the omelet onto a warm plate; cover to keep warm. Repeat with the
remaining olive oil and tofu mixture to make a second omelet; slide onto
a second warm plate.

3   Make the spinach filling. Put the spinach leaves, shallot, tomatoes, red
wine vinegar, and olive oil in a medium bowl; toss gently to combine.
Top with the vegan feta.

4   Divide the filling between the omelets, placing it over half of each
omelet; fold over the omelets to cover the filling.

marinated vegan feta Put 3/4 cup (115g) raw cashews and 3/4 cup (105g)
raw macadamias in a bowl with enough water to cover; allow to stand for
8 hours or overnight. Drain the nuts; rinse well. Process the nuts with
1 tablespoon nutritional yeast flakes, 1 teaspoon sea salt flakes, 1/4 cup
(60ml) lemon juice, and 1/4 cup (60ml) olive oil until smooth. Press the
mixture firmly into a 9 x 6-inch (23 x 15cm) baking dish lined with plastic
wrap. When firm, turn the tofu out onto a parchment paper–lined baking
sheet. Preheat the oven to 400°F (200°C). Bake for 20 minutes or until
golden. Allow to cool, then cut into squares. Store in a glass jar or similar,
covered in olive oil, with sprigs of fresh rosemary and thyme, and peeled
garlic cloves. The marinated feta will keep in the fridge for up to 2 weeks.
(Makes about 220g)

Avocado toast with smoky chickpeas

PREP + COOK TIME **15 MINUTES** | SERVES **2**

Simple to put together but brimming with flavor, this easy breakfast will kick-start your day with good portions of protein, fiber, and healthy fats. Chickpeas and avocado are nutrient-rich, providing essential vitamins and minerals such as manganese, folate, and potassium.

1 cup (190g) rinsed and drained canned chickpeas (see tips)

2 tbsp olive oil

1/2 tsp sea salt flakes

1/2 tsp smoked paprika

1/2 tsp ground cumin

4 slices of wholegrain sourdough bread, toasted

1 large avocado (320g), mashed

1/3 cup (15g) microgreens (see tips)

2 tbsp sriracha

lime wedges, to serve

1 Pat the chickpeas dry with paper towels. Heat the olive oil in a large skillet over high heat. Add the chickpeas and salt; cook, stirring occasionally, for 5 minutes. Add the smoked paprika and cumin; cook, stirring, for a further 30 seconds.

2 Spread the sourdough toast with the mashed avocado. Top with the smoky chickpeas and microgreens; drizzle with the sriracha. Serve with lime wedges.

TIPS

- The drained liquid from the chickpeas, called aquafaba, can be used to make vegan meringue (see Frozen No-Bake Blueberry and Lime Meringue Slab on page 158). Aquafaba can be stored in a container in the fridge for 2 days or frozen for up to 3 months.
- Instead of the microgreens, you can use cilantro or any full-sized chopped soft-leaf herb such as flat-leaf parsley, dill, or mint.

Maple butternut waffles with pecans

PREP + COOK TIME **1 HOUR + STANDING** | SERVES **4**

This vegan waffle recipe is a jaw-dropping way to start (or end) your day. With the sweetness of squash and maple syrup, and the buttery toastiness of pecans, it's a dream come true. Butternut is the best variety of winter squash to use here, as it has dry, dense flesh.

$1^1/_3$ cups (200g) white spelt flour

2 tsp baking powder

$^1/_2$ tsp sea salt flakes

1 tsp ground cinnamon

$^1/_2$ tsp ground allspice

$^1/_2$ tsp ground nutmeg

$^3/_4$ cup (180ml) almond milk

$^1/_4$ cup (60ml) olive oil

$^1/_2$ cup (120g) mashed cooked butternut squash (see tip)

2 tbsp pure maple syrup, plus extra to serve

2 tsp vanilla extract

nonstick cooking spray

4 scoops of dairy-free vanilla ice cream

$^2/_3$ cup (80g) coarsely chopped pecans, roasted

1　Sift together the flour, baking powder, salt, cinnamon, allspice, and nutmeg in a large bowl. In a separate bowl, combine the almond milk, olive oil, mashed squash, maple syrup, and vanilla until smooth.

2　Pour the pumpkin mixture into the flour mixture; stir until just combined but still with some lumps. Allow the batter to stand for 10 minutes.

3　Preheat the waffle iron according to the manufacturer's instructions; spray with a little cooking spray.

4　Gently stir the batter. Pour $^1/_4$ cup (60ml) of the batter onto the center of each square section of the waffle iron to just cover the bottom. Close the lid; cook for 3 minutes or until golden brown. Transfer to a wire rack. Repeat with the remaining batter to make a total of 8 waffles.

5　Serve the waffles topped with the scoops of ice cream, chopped pecans, and extra maple syrup.

TIP

For mashed squash, cook 2 cups (180g) peeled, seeded, chopped squash with 1 tablespoon water, in a microwave-safe bowl covered with plastic wrap, on high power for 8 minutes or until tender; mash. Alternatively, steam the squash in a steamer over a saucepan of simmering water until tender; mash.

Crushed pea and pickled vegetable toast

PREP + COOK TIME **15 MINUTES** | SERVES **4**

Pickled vegetables such as kimchi and sauerkraut are traditionally preserved using lactic acid fermentation. Eating fermented foods adds live microbes to the existing colony of microbes that live in our guts, contributing to good and balanced health.

3 cups (360g) frozen green peas

$\frac{1}{3}$ cup (90g) hulled tahini

2 tbsp fresh dill leaves

1 garlic clove, crushed

2 tbsp lemon juice

1 tbsp Dijon mustard

2 tbsp sunflower seeds

2 tsp sesame seeds

2 tsp flaxseeds

8 slices of sprouted bread, toasted

$1\frac{1}{3}$ cups (240g) drained fermented vegetables of choice

1 cup (15g) loosely packed pea shoots or alfalfa sprouts

salt and freshly ground black pepper

$\frac{1}{2}$ lemon, cut into 4 wedges

1 Put the peas in a heatproof bowl; cover with boiling water. Allow to stand for 2 minutes; drain. Blend or process the peas, tahini, dill, garlic, lemon juice, and Dijon mustard until a chunky spread forms. Season with salt and pepper to taste.

2 Put the sunflower seeds, sesame seeds, and flaxseeds in a small heavy-bottomed skillet. Toast the seeds over medium-high heat, stirring constantly, until lightly browned.

3 Top the toasted bread with the pea spread, fermented vegetables, toasted seeds, and pea shoots. Serve with the lemon wedges.

TIPS

- Hulled tahini, which has the hull of the sesame seed removed, will have a smoother texture than its unhulled counterpart.
- The pea spread can be kept in an airtight container in the fridge for up to 1 day. Toast the bread and assemble the toasts just before serving.

Almond milk and mango pikelets

PREP + COOK TIME **25 MINUTES + STANDING** | SERVES **4**

Pikelets are a cross between silver-dollar pancakes and crumpets with a heavier texture than regular pancakes. You can choose a different seasonal fruit, if you'd like, or turn this into a dessert by topping the pikelets with scoops of dairy-free vanilla ice cream.

$1^2/_3$ cups (225g) all-purpose flour

2 tsp baking powder

$^1/_4$ tsp salt

1 tbsp coconut sugar

$1^1/_2$ cups (375ml) almond milk

1 tbsp coconut oil, melted

$^1/_2$ tsp vanilla extract

$^1/_4$ cup (55g) firmly packed vegan brown sugar

2 small mangoes (600g), sliced

$^1/_3$ cup (25g) sliced almonds, toasted (optional; see tip)

1 Sift the flour, baking powder, salt, and sugar into a medium bowl. Gradually whisk in the almond milk, coconut oil, and vanilla extract until smooth. Allow to stand for 15 minutes.

2 Heat a large nonstick skillet over medium heat. Using 2 tablespoons of batter for each pikelet, cook about 4 pikelets at a time for 2 minutes or until bubbles appear on the surface. Turn; cook on the other side until golden. Remove the pikelets from the pan; cover to keep warm. Repeat with the remaining batter to make 12 pikelets in total.

3 Heat $^1/_2$ cup (125ml) water and the brown sugar in a medium skillet over low heat, stirring, until the sugar has dissolved. Bring to the boil. Boil, uncovered, for 3 minutes or until the syrup thickens slightly.

4 Serve the warm pikelets with the mango, syrup, and toasted almonds, if you'd like.

TIP

Toasting nuts brings out the flavor. There are two ways to toast them: Spread the nuts onto a baking sheet; roast in a 350°F (180°C) oven for 5–10 minutes until the nuts are golden brown (stir once during roasting for even cooking). Or, put the nuts in a heavy-bottomed skillet; stir continuously over medium heat until evenly browned.

PACK AND GO

Appetizing snacks, appealing lunches, nutritious, quick-to-put-together options for busy lifestyles—and all ideal for eating at home or taking with you when on the go.

Cauliflower dip with rice crackers

PREP + COOK TIME **1 HOUR 30 MINUTES + SOAKING** | SERVES **4 (MAKES 3 CUPS)**

Roasting cauliflower allows it to caramelize, bringing out its earthy flavor and natural sweetness—particularly when it is paired with earthy spice mixes such as dukkah. Serve with crudités such as sliced cucumber, radishes, and baby carrots.

1 lb (400g) cauliflower, cut into florets

1/4 cup (60ml) olive oil, divided

2 tbsp dukkah, divided

3 garlic cloves, unpeeled

1/2 cup (140g) dairy-free yogurt

1 (15.5 oz/439g) can cannellini beans, drained, rinsed

2 tbsp lemon juice

1/4 cup (35g) coarsely chopped roasted hazelnuts

salt and freshly ground black pepper

rice crackers

1/4 cup (45g) flaxseeds

1/3 cup (70g) red quinoa, rinsed

1 cup (175g) cooked brown rice (see tips)

1 tsp sea salt

2 tsp tamari

1 1/2 tbsp olive oil

1/3 cup (50g) sesame seeds, toasted

TIPS

- The crackers can be made a week ahead. Store in an airtight container until needed.
- You can use precooked brown rice for this recipe, or boil about 1/3 cup (65g) uncooked brown rice.

1 First, make the rice crackers. Put the flaxseeds in a small bowl; add enough water to cover. Allow to stand for at least 20 minutes. Drain well, then dry with paper towels.

2 Meanwhile, put the quinoa and 2 cups (500ml) water in a small saucepan; bring to the boil. Simmer, uncovered, for 12 minutes or until tender. Drain well; allow to cool.

3 Blend or process the flaxseeds, quinoa, rice, sea salt, tamari, and olive oil in a food processor until the mixture forms a ball; add 1 tablespoon water, if needed, to bring it together. Add the sesame seeds; pulse to combine. The dough will be very sticky.

4 Preheat the oven to 400°F (200°C). Divide the dough in half. Roll each half between 2 sheets of parchment paper until 1/8 inch (2mm) thick. Remove the top layer of parchment. Using a knife, score the top of the dough into desired shapes; slide, still on the parchment, onto baking sheets. Bake for 40 minutes or until crisp and golden. Allow to cool for 5 minutes; break the crackers along the score lines. Cool completely.

5 To make the cauliflower dip, preheat the oven to 425°F (220°C). Line a baking sheet with parchment paper.

6 Place the cauliflower on the prepared baking sheet. Drizzle with half of the olive oil; sprinkle with 1 tablespoon of the dukkah. Toss to coat. Add the garlic to the same tray. Roast for 30 minutes or until tender. Allow to cool to room temperature. Remove the garlic from the peels.

7 Process the cauliflower, garlic, yogurt, cannellini beans, lemon juice, and remaining olive oil until smooth. Season with salt and pepper to taste. Transfer to a serving bowl. Sprinkle with the hazelnuts and the remaining 1 tablespoon dukkah.

8 Serve the dip with the crackers and crudités, if you'd like. Season with salt and pepper to taste.

Sweet potato and black bean roll ups

PREP + COOK TIME **1 HOUR 5 MINUTES** | MAKES **12**

A meat-free variation on a family favorite, these roll-up pastries pack a flavor punch. With good carbohydrates, fiber, and protein from the sweet potatoes and black beans, they are nutritious and filling. Great straight from the oven, they also make an ideal portable lunch.

$1^2/_3$ lb (750g) sweet potatoes, peeled, cut into 1-in (2.5cm) cubes

$^1/_2$ cup (170g) finely chopped red onion

olive oil cooking spray

1 (15 oz/400g) can black beans, drained, rinsed

$^1/_3$ cup (20g) coarsely chopped flat-leaf parsley

$^1/_4$ cup (40g) pine nuts, toasted, coarsely chopped

3 oz (100g) marinated or herbed vegan feta, crumbled (see tips)

2 sheets (490g) of frozen vegan puff pastry, just thawed

1 tbsp soy milk

2 tsp black sesame seeds

2 tsp white sesame seeds

1 cup (320g) tomato chutney (see tips)

salt and freshly ground black pepper

1 Preheat the oven to 350°F (180°C). Line 2 baking sheets with parchment paper.

2 Place the sweet potatoes and onion on one of the trays. Lightly spray with the olive oil; season with salt and pepper to taste. Roast for 30 minutes or until the sweet potatoes are soft. Allow to cool slightly. Increase the oven temperature to 450°F (230°C).

3 Put the roasted sweet potatoes and onion in a large bowl with the black beans; lightly crush using a fork. Add the parsley and pine nuts; mix well. Gently fold in the feta.

4 Cut the puff pastry sheets in half. Place a quarter of the filling mixture along one long edge; brush the opposite edge with a little of the soy milk. Roll up to enclose the filling. Cut the roll into 3 pieces; place seam-side down on the second lined tray. Repeat with the remaining pastry and filling mixture to make 12 sausage rolls.

5 Brush the tops of the rolls with the remaining soy milk; sprinkle with the combined sesame seeds.

6 Bake the sausage rolls for 30 minutes or until golden brown. Serve hot or at room temperature, accompanied by the chutney.

TIPS

- You can make the marinated vegan feta on page 38 and use it in this recipe instead of buying it.
- Use spiced tofu instead of vegan feta, if you'd like.
- You can use salsa or even ketchup in place of the chutney if preferred.

Tofu banh mi rolls

PREP + COOK TIME **15 MINUTES** | MAKES **2**

Vietnamese banh mi rolls are a popular street food often eaten for breakfast or as a snack. Fillings vary, but all reflect the fusion of Vietnamese ingredients with French-style baguettes and condiments such as mayonnaise. Use crusty, baguette-like bread rolls for best results.

2 cups (150g) undressed coleslaw salad mix (see tips)

$^1/_4$ cup (7g) fresh cilantro leaves

$^1/_4$ cup (75g) vegan mayonnaise (use the recipe for Everyday Mayo at right or use store-bought), divided

2 tsp rice wine vinegar

$^1/_2$ tsp sesame oil

$^1/_2$ tsp sea salt flakes

1 tsp olive oil

8 oz (225) satay marinated tofu (see tips)

2 crusty mini-baguettes or sandwich rolls

1 Put the coleslaw salad mix and cilantro in a medium bowl. Add 1 tablespoon of the vegan mayonnaise, the rice wine vinegar, sesame oil, and sea salt; toss to coat well.

2 Heat the olive oil in a medium skillet over medium-high heat; cook the marinated tofu for 2 minutes on each side or until golden and heated through.

3 Split the bread in half lengthwise; spread both sides with the remaining mayonnaise. Fill with the fried tofu and coleslaw mixture.

everyday mayo Drain all liquid (aquafaba) from 1 (15 oz/425g) can chickpeas; you will need $^1/_4$ cup (60ml) aquafaba. Blend the reserved aquafaba with 1 tablespoon apple cider vinegar, $^1/_2$ teaspoon sea salt flakes, and $^1/_2$ teaspoon Dijon mustard in a small blender (do not use a food processor) until smooth. With the motor operating, add $^1/_2$ cup (125ml) olive oil in a slow, steady stream until thick and creamy. (The mayonnaise will thicken further in the fridge.) Spoon the mayonnaise into a screw-top jar with a tight-fitting lid. Store in the fridge for up to 2 weeks. (Makes 2 cups/500ml)

spicy mayonnaise Make the Everyday Mayo as above. Stir in 1 teaspoon smoked paprika, 2 teaspoons tomato paste, 1 crushed garlic clove, and $^1/_4$ teaspoon chili flakes. Serve with the vegan burgers on page 132 or anything to which you'd like to add a little kick of smoky, spicy flavor.

turmeric mayonnaise First make the Everyday Mayo. Stir in $^1/_2$ teaspoon ground turmeric, 2 tablespoons finely grated carrot, 2 tablespoons white miso paste (shiro miso), and 1 tablespoon sesame oil. This mayonnaise works well with most things.

TIPS

• You can make your own coleslaw mix using a combination of red and white cabbage, carrot, and even beets.

• You can use Asian-style marinated tofu instead of satay-flavored. To make your own satay marinated tofu, combine 1 cup (260g) crunchy peanut butter, 1 tablespoon kecap manis (sweet soy sauce) or coconut aminos, and 2 teaspoons peanut oil with 8 oz (225g) firm tofu; refrigerate for 20 minutes before cooking.

Beet monster munch balls

PREP + COOK TIME **20 MINUTES + REFRIGERATION** | MAKES **28**

These beet-red, slightly crunchy, chewy, and sweet protein balls are a perfect snack on the go or can be served with herbal tea or freshly squeezed juice. As an energy-rich treat, they also make a great pre- or post-workout snack.

1 cup (160g) raw almonds

1 cup (140g) dried dates, pitted

1 lb (400g) raw red beets, trimmed, peeled, finely grated

1/2 cup (60g) goji berries

1/4 cup (40g) chia seeds

1/4 cup (25g) cacao powder

1/4 cup (35g) lucuma powder (see tips)

1 tbsp whole psyllium husks

1/2 cup (80g) activated buckinis (see tips on page 28)

1/4 cup (90g) rice malt syrup

freeze-dried raspberries (optional), crushed

1 In the bowl of a food processor, process the almonds and dates until slightly coarse crumbs form; transfer to a large bowl. Add the remaining ingredients, except for the raspberries; mix well with your hands until combined. (You could use disposable gloves to protect your hands from staining from the beets.)

2 Roll 1 tablespoon of the mixture into a ball; roll in the crushed freeze-dried raspberries, if using. You will need to press the raspberry coating into the ball slightly to help it stick. Place the coated ball on a tray; repeat with the remaining mixture.

3 Cover the protein balls on the tray, then refrigerate for 4 hours or until firm. Transfer to an airtight container.

TIPS

- Lucuma powder, ground from a Peruvian fruit, has a creamy, citrus flavor. It's available from some health food stores or can be ordered online.
- Roll the protein balls in chopped nuts such as pistachios, sifted cacao powder, goji berries, or toasted shredded coconut instead of the freeze-dried raspberries, if you'd like.
- These protein balls will keep in an airtight container for up to 1 week in the fridge or can be frozen for up to 2 months; they can be eaten straight from the freezer.

Mexican quinoa pots

PREP + COOK TIME **35 MINUTES** | SERVES **2**

Make the pots with white, red, or tri-colored quinoa, or use other whole grains such as barley or farro. Assembling the salad in jars makes it simple to transport for lunch at work, for instance, but you can use any container you'd like for convenience.

1/2 cup (100g) white quinoa, rinsed

1 ear of corn (350g), husks and silks removed

1 (15 oz/425g) can black beans, drained, rinsed

1 small red bell pepper (150g), finely chopped

2 green onions, thinly sliced

1 1/2 tbsp olive oil

2 tbsp lime juice, divided

1 fresh long red chile, thinly sliced, divided

1 small avocado (200g)

1 small garlic clove, crushed

2 sprigs of cilantro

2 lime wedges

salt and freshly ground black pepper

tortilla chips, to serve (optional)

1 Put the quinoa and 2 cups (500ml) water in a small saucepan over medium-high heat; bring to a boil. Reduce the heat to low; simmer for 12 minutes or until tender. Drain; rinse under cold water.

2 Heat a ridged cast-iron grill pan over high heat. Cook the corn cob, rotating so that it cooks all over, for 12 minutes or until lightly charred. Allow to cool slightly, then cut the kernels from the cob.

3 Put the cooked quinoa and corn kernels in a medium bowl with the black beans, red bell pepper, green onion, olive oil, half of the lime juice, and half of the chile; stir to combine. Season with salt and pepper to taste.

4 Place avocado, garlic, and remaining lime juice in a small bowl; mash to combine. Season the guacamole with salt and pepper to taste.

5 To assemble the jars, spoon the quinoa mixture into the bottom of two (3-cup/750-ml) jars. Top with the guacamole, cilantro sprigs, remaining chile, and a lime wedge. Serve with tortilla chips, if you'd like.

TIP

Use canned red kidney beans instead of black beans, if preferred.

Bento box

PREP + COOK TIME **1 HOUR** | SERVES **4**

Bento is the Japanese answer to a packed lunch. Usually based on rice or noodles, it is a balanced meal for one, containing carbohydrates, protein, and pickled or cooked vegetables. Our bento box is made up of nori rolls with edamame for contrasting crunch.

1 cup (200g) sushi rice (uncooked)

3 tbsp rice vinegar

1 tbsp sugar

$^1/_4$ tsp salt

2 large roma tomatoes (180g)

2 tbsp soy sauce

1 tbsp ground dried wakame (see tips)

2 tsp grated fresh ginger

2 tsp sriracha

1 tsp sesame oil

3 nori sheets (10g)

$^1/_2$ small avocado (100g), cubed

$^1/_2$ small seedless cucumber (50g),
cut into $^1/_2$-in (1.25cm) matchsticks

$1^1/_2$ cups (80g) frozen edamame, blanched

2 tbsp pink pickled ginger

1 tsp sesame seeds, toasted

$^1/_4$ cup soy sauce

1 tbsp vegan mayonnaise
(see Everyday Mayo on page 55 or use store-bought)

1 Put the rice in a sieve; rinse under cold running water until the water runs clear. Put the rinsed rice in a saucepan with $1^1/_2$ cups (375ml) water; bring to a boil. Reduce the heat to low; cook, covered, for 10 minutes or until the water is absorbed. Remove the pan from the heat; allow to stand, covered, for 15 minutes. Meanwhile, in a small bowl, combine the rice vinegar, sugar, and salt. Stir until dissolved. While the rice is still hot, add the vinegar mixture; stir with a fork for 5 minutes or until the rice is sticky and slightly cooled.

2 Score a cross into the bottom of each tomato; place in a heatproof bowl. Pour in boiling water to cover; allow to stand for 1 minute or until the skins start to peel away. Using a slotted spoon, transfer the tomatoes to a bowl of iced water. When cool enough to handle, peel away the skins.

3 Cut the tomatoes in half; scoop out the seeds and discard. Cut the flesh into $^1/_2$-inch (1.25cm) pieces.

4 In another bowl, whisk together the soy sauce, ground wakame, ginger, sriracha, and sesame oil until combined. Add the tomato; stir to coat. Allow to stand for 30 minutes.

5 To make the rolls, place the nori sheet, shiny-side down, on a sushi mat with the long side in front of you. Using damp hands, spread 1 cup of the cooled sticky rice over the nori, leaving a 1 inch (2.5cm) strip at the top. Place one-third of the tomato mixture, avocado, and cucumber across the center of the rice. Using the sushi mat, roll up firmly away from you. Dampen the nori strip lightly and seal. Repeat twice more with the remaining ingredients to make 3 nori rolls.

6 Cut each nori roll into 6 pieces. Serve the nori rolls with the edamame, pickled ginger, sesame seeds, soy sauce, and vegan mayonnaise.

TIPS

- Use a spice grinder or high-powered mini food processor to grind the seaweed to a coarse powder.
- You will need a sushi mat to roll the sushi.

Samosa wraps

PREP + COOK TIME **30 MINUTES** | SERVES **2**

The filling for these wraps is inspired by classic potato-and-pea samosas, right
down to the accompanying chutney. Mix it up by using sweet potato and different varieties
of wraps and chutney, if you'd like.

1 large russet potato (300g), peeled, cut into ½-in (1.25cm) pieces

2 tbsp olive oil

½ cup (60g) frozen green peas

2 tsp curry powder

2 (6-in/15cm) flaxseed, chia, quinoa, or other whole-grain wraps

2 tbsp vegan mayonnaise (see Everyday Mayo on page 55 or use store-bought)

1 cup (30g) baby spinach leaves

1 cucumber (130g), thinly sliced lengthwise

¼ cup (60g) thinly sliced red onion

⅓ cup (10g) cilantro leaves

2 tbsp mango chutney

½ lime, cut into wedges

1 Boil, steam, or microwave the potato until just tender; drain.

2 Heat the olive oil in a medium skillet over high heat; cook the potato, green peas, and curry powder, stirring constantly, for 3 minutes or until the potatoes are slightly mashed and the peas are hot.

3 Spread the wraps with the mayonnaise; top with the spinach leaves, cucumber, onion, cilantro, potato mixture, and chutney. Roll up to enclose the filling. Serve with the lime wedges.

TIPS

- These wraps can be enjoyed warm or cold. For cold wraps, remember to allow the potato filling to cool before assembling.
- Cover the assembled wraps in plastic wrap and refrigerate until ready to eat.
- If you would like to eat these warm but are making them ahead of time, keep the filling and wraps separate; warm the potato filling just before assembling and eating. The potato mixture will keep, refrigerated, for up to 3 days.

Zucchini and kale frittatas

PREP + COOK TIME **50 MINUTES** | MAKES **12**

Turmeric and ginger are both powerful anti-inflammatories that aid in the digestion of fats, while leafy greens such as kale provide the vegan eater with an arsenal of nutrients—iron, calcium, and an array of valuable vitamins.

olive oil cooking spray

1 lb (480g) small zucchini (about 4), divided

2 tbsp olive oil

$\frac{1}{2}$ cup (150g) finely chopped onion

$\frac{1}{2}$ tsp cumin seeds, crushed

$\frac{1}{2}$ tsp fennel seeds, crushed

2 garlic cloves, crushed

2 tbsp grated fresh ginger

$\frac{3}{4}$ lb (350g) purple kale

10 oz (300g) firm tofu, drained of excess liquid

$\frac{1}{2}$ cup (125ml) soy milk

$\frac{1}{3}$ cup (55g) whole wheat flour

2 tbsp nutritional yeast flakes

1 tsp ground turmeric

vegan mayonnaise (see Everyday Mayo on page 55 or use store-bought), to serve

1 Preheat the oven to 325°F (160°C). Grease a 12-hole ($\frac{1}{3}$-cup/80ml) muffin tin; line the bottoms and sides with overlapping squares of parchment paper.

2 Coarsely grate 3 of the zucchini; place in the middle of a piece of muslin, then twist the ends of the cloth to wring out any excess liquid. (Alternatively, pick up small handfuls of zucchini, and squeeze tightly to remove the excess liquid.) Set aside.

3 Heat the olive oil in a skillet over medium heat; cook the onion, cumin seeds, and fennel seeds, stirring, for 4 minutes or until the onion softens. Add the garlic and ginger; cook for a further minute or until fragrant.

4 Strip the kale leaves from the stem; discard the stems. (You will need $\frac{1}{2}$ lb or 225g kale leaves.) Coarsely chop two-thirds of the leaves. Add the chopped kale and grated zucchini to the pan with the onion mixture; cook for a further 2 minutes. Allow to cool.

5 Meanwhile, in a food processor, process the tofu, soy milk, flour, nutritional yeast flakes, and turmeric until smooth.

6 Combine the tofu mixture and zucchini mixture in a large bowl. Ladle the mixture into the prepared holes of the muffin tin. Using a vegetable peeler, peel the remaining zucchini into long, thin ribbons. Roll up the ribbons; top the frittatas with the remaining kale leaves and zucchini rolls. Spray with olive oil cooking spray.

7 Bake the frittatas for 20 minutes or until golden and firm. Serve with vegan mayonnaise.

TIPS

- Instead of purple kale, use the same weight of curly kale or Tuscan kale (also known as Lacinato).
- Increase your iron absorption by serving the frittatas with a wedge of lemon.

Tamari noodle jars

PREP + COOK TIME **20 MINUTES** | SERVES **2**

Tamari is similar to soy sauce but thicker and more balanced in flavor. As part of the tamari
sesame dressing, it brings a great flavor to this easy-to-assemble layered noodle salad.
The vegetables stay crisp, and it's easy to toss when it's time to eat.

3.5 oz (100g) dried rice stick noodles

8 oz (225g) firm tofu, cubed

1 cup (80g) finely shredded red cabbage

2 small carrots (140g), julienned or grated

2 tbsp kimchi (see tip)

1 cup (80g) beansprouts

1/2 cup (15g) cilantro leaves

1/2 cup (10g) mint leaves

tamari sesame dressing

2 1/2 in (6cm) piece of fresh ginger

2 tbsp tamari

1 tbsp sesame oil

1 tbsp olive oil

1 tbsp rice wine vinegar

1 Cook the noodles in a medium saucepan of boiling water for 6 minutes
or until tender. Drain; rinse under running cold water. Set aside.

2 Make the tamari sesame dressing. Peel and finely grate the ginger.
Squeeze the grated ginger in your hand over a small bowl to extract the
juice; you should have about 1 teaspoon ginger juice. Discard the ginger
pulp. Add the remaining ingredients to the bowl; mix to combine.

3 Place the tofu cubes into 2 (3 1/2-cup/875ml) jars with a lid; pour the
dressing over the tofu. Layer with the cabbage, carrot, noodles, kimchi,
and beansprouts, then top with the cilantro and mint. Cover the jars with
their lids. Refrigerate until ready to eat.

4 To serve, pour the contents into a bowl, and toss to combine.

TIPS

- A julienne peeler looks like a wide-bladed
vegetable peeler with a serrated rather than straight
blade. They are available from kitchenware stores
and Asian grocers. Alternatively, cut the carrot into
julienne using a mandoline or sharp knife.
- If you don't have kimchi, toss the cabbage in
1 teaspoon rice wine vinegar before layering.

Real "instant" noodles

Once you have these homemade "instant' noodles in your repertoire, you may never reach
for packaged instant noodles again. Chock-full of flavor, freshness, and all-round goodness,
they leave their prepackaged compatriots in the shade.

Tofu tom yum

PREP + COOK TIME **5 MINUTES** | SERVES **1**

Place 1 teaspoon vegetarian tom yum paste in a 2-cup (500ml) heatproof jar with a fitted lid. Add $^3/_4$ oz (20g) dried rice vermicelli noodles, 3 halved cherry tomatoes, 2 oz (60g) diced tofu, 2 torn oyster mushrooms, 1 tablespoon fresh ginger cut into matchsticks, 1 torn fresh makrut lime leaf, 1 tablespoon beansprouts, and a small handful of cilantro leaves. To serve, pour in $1^1/_2$ cups (375ml) boiling water; stir to combine. Cover with the lid; allow to stand for 3 minutes. Serve with a lime wedge for squeezing over.

Miso ramen noodles

PREP + COOK TIME **5 MINUTES** | SERVES **1**

Stir together 2 teaspoons white miso paste (shiro miso), 1 teaspoon sesame oil, and 1 teaspoon grated fresh ginger in a 2-cup (500ml) heatproof jar with a fitted lid. Top with 2 oz (50g) cubed silken tofu, $^1/_4$ small (17g) carrot julienned, 3 oz (90g) ramen noodles, $^1/_4$ cup shelled and thawed edamame beans, and $^1/_4$ cup (25g) enoki mushrooms. To serve, pour in $1^1/_2$ cups (375ml) boiling water; stir to combine. Cover with the lid; allow to stand for 3 minutes. Serve topped with 1 green onion sliced on the diagonal.

Green curry noodles

PREP + COOK TIME **5 MINUTES** | SERVES **1**

Stir together $1^1/_2$ tablespoons vegan green curry paste and $^1/_4$ cup (60ml) coconut cream in a 2-cup (500ml) heatproof jar with a fitted lid. Top with $^1/_2$ oz (10g) brown (or white) rice vermicelli noodles, $^1/_4$ cup (20g) small broccoli florets, 2 tablespoons frozen green peas, $^1/_4$ cup (10g) baby spinach leaves, and 1 thinly sliced green onion. To serve, pour in $1^1/_2$ cups (375ml) boiling water; stir to combine. Cover with the lid; allow to stand for 3 minutes.

Thai curry laksa

PREP + COOK TIME **5 MINUTES** | SERVES **1**

Stir together $1^1/_2$ tablespoons vegan red curry paste and $^1/_4$ cup (60ml) coconut cream in a 2-cup (500ml) heatproof jar with a fitted lid. Top with $^1/_2$ cup (25g) coarsely shredded Asian greens (such as bok choy, bamboo shoots, beansprouts, or napa cabbage), $^1/_4$ cup (20g) snow peas, $^3/_4$ oz (20g) fresh thin rice noodles, and $^1/_4$ cup (35g) fried tofu. To serve, pour in $1^1/_2$ cups (375ml) boiling water; stir to combine. Cover with the lid; allow to stand for 3 minutes. Serve topped with 1 tablespoon each of fried shallots and Thai basil leaves.

Mushroom and spinach flatbread

PREP + COOK TIME **15 MINUTES** | MAKES **4**

Traditionally, this filled Turkish flatbread is made from hand-rolled dough, but this super-quick version uses premade wraps instead. Don't forget the squeeze of lemon juice—it makes a big difference and ensures your flatbread will be at its best!

$^1/_3$ cup (80ml) olive oil, divided

$^1/_4$ cup (80g) finely chopped onion

2 garlic cloves, crushed

2 tsp ground cumin

2 tsp ground sumac

$^1/_2$ tsp chili flakes

$^3/_4$ lb (350g) portabella mushrooms, thickly sliced

3.5 oz (100g) vegan cheddar, grated

2 cups (60g) spinach leaves

2 tbsp pine nuts, toasted

4 (8-in/20cm) whole grain or seed wraps

olive oil cooking spray

salt and freshly ground black pepper

dill leaves and lemon wedges, to serve

1 Heat 1 tablespoon of the olive oil in a large skillet over high heat; cook the onion and garlic, stirring, for 5 minutes or until softened. Stir in the cumin, sumac, and chili flakes; cook for 1 minute. Transfer the mixture to a bowl.

2 Heat $1^1/_2$ tablespoons of the olive oil in the same skillet. Add half of the mushrooms; cook, turning occasionally, for 5 minutes or until golden. Add the cooked mushrooms to the onion mixture. Repeat with the remaining oil and mushrooms. Allow the combined mixture to cool for 10 minutes. Stir in the vegan cheddar, spinach, and pine nuts; season with salt and pepper to taste.

3 Wipe out the same skillet, then heat over high heat. Place 2 wraps on a clean work surface. Spread a quarter of the filling mixture down the center third of each wrap. Fold both sides over to enclose. Spray with olive oil cooking spray. Cook in the pan for 2 minutes on each side or until the cheddar melts and the bread is crisp. Using a large spatula, remove from the pan. Cover to keep warm. Repeat with the remaining wraps and filling, spraying with olive oil as needed.

4 Cut each flatbread diagonally, and serve with dill leaves and lemon wedges for squeezing over.

TIP

If you have one, use a sandwich press to cook these super-easy flatbreads (as pictured here). Follow steps 1 and 2 as in the method, then sandwich the filling between the wraps to make 2 large stuffed flatbreads. Cook in the preheated sandwich press until golden and crisp. Cut into wedges to serve.

Tuscan kale and lentil salad with tempeh chips

PREP + COOK TIME **25 MINUTES** | SERVES **4**

Green lentils are related to the famous French lentils du Puy; these tiny green-blue lentils have a nutty, earthy flavor and a hardy nature that allows them to be rapidly cooked without disintegrating. Green lentils similarly hold their shape well.

1³/₄ cups (350g) dried green lentils (see tips)

10 Tuscan kale leaves (100g), trimmed, shredded

1 lb (400g) mixed baby tomatoes, halved

¹/₄ cup (80g) thinly sliced red onion

¹/₄ cup (7g) loosely packed small basil leaves

¹/₄ cup (5g) loosely packed mint leaves

¹/₄ cup (5g) loosely packed flat-leaf parsley leaves

¹/₂ cup (125ml) olive oil

¹/₄ cup (60ml) red wine vinegar

2 tsp Dijon mustard

salt and freshly ground black pepper

tempeh chips

¹/₄ cup (60ml) olive oil

3.5oz (100g) tempeh, cut into ¹/₄-in (6mm) thick slices

1 Cook the lentils in a large saucepan of boiling water, uncovered, for 12 minutes or until just tender; drain. Rinse under cold water; drain well.

2 Meanwhile, make the tempeh chips. Heat the olive oil in a large skillet over medium-high heat; cook the tempeh for 1 minute on each side or until golden. Drain on paper towels.

3 Arrange the lentils, kale, tomatoes, onion, and herbs on 4 serving plates or trays.

4 To make the dressing, put the olive oil, red wine vinegar, and Dijon mustard in a screw-top jar with a tight-fitting lid; shake well. Season with salt and pepper to taste.

5 Serve the salad with the tempeh chips and the dressing in small bowls on the side.

TIPS

- You can use a mixture of green lentils and Puy lentils, if you'd like.
- Tuscan kale is also known as Lacinato or cavolo nero. You can use other leafy greens such as kale, Swiss chard, or even spinach instead.
- Tempeh, made from fermented soybeans, can be found in the refrigerator section of the store.

Sweet potato and pea samosas

PREP + COOK TIME **50 MINUTES** | MAKES **8**

Make your own delectable samosa-style pastries filled with spiced sweet potato. You can also make these fragrant, crispy triangles with regular potatoes, or use a mixture of potato and sweet potato, if you'd like.

1 lb (450g) sweet potatoes, peeled, cut into 1/2-in (1cm) cubes

2 tbsp coconut oil, melted, divided (see tips)

1/4 cup (80g) finely chopped onion

2 tsp grated fresh ginger

2 tsp curry powder

1 cup (120g) frozen green peas

1/3 cup (50g) sunflower seeds

8 sheets of phyllo pastry (180g)

1/2 tsp cumin seeds

1/2 tsp sea salt flakes

salt and freshly ground black pepper

lemon wedges, to serve

mint apple raita

1/2 cup (10g) mint leaves

1/4 tsp sea salt flakes

1 cup (280g) coconut yogurt (use Homemade Coconut Yogurt on page 21 or purchase premade)

1 small green apple (130g), julienned

TIPS

- Use olive oil instead of coconut oil, if you'd like.
- You can also cook the samosas in a flat sandwich press for 2 minutes or until crisp and lightly golden.

1 Preheat the oven to 400°F (200°C). Line a baking sheet with parchment paper.

2 Put the sweet potato in a medium saucepan with enough water to cover; bring to a boil over high heat. Boil for 5 minutes or until just tender. Drain well.

3 Heat half of the coconut oil in a skillet over medium heat; cook the onion, ginger, and curry powder, stirring, for 3 minutes or until fragrant and softened. Add the sweet potato and peas; cook, stirring, for 1 minute or until the liquid evaporates. Stir in the sunflower seeds; season with salt and pepper to taste. Allow to cool.

4 Brush 1 sheet of the phyllo pastry with a little of the remaining coconut oil. Fold in half lengthwise, then brush with a little more coconut oil. Place 1/3 cup of the sweet potato mixture at the bottom of one narrow edge of the folded pastry sheet. Fold one corner of the pastry diagonally over the filling to form a triangle. Continue folding to the end of the pastry sheet, retaining the triangular shape. Place on the prepared baking sheet; brush with a little more coconut oil. Repeat with the remaining phyllo, coconut oil, and filling mixture to make a total of 8 samosas. Sprinkle with the cumin seeds and sea salt flakes.

5 Bake the samosas for 15 minutes or until golden and crisp.

6 Make the mint apple raita. Using a mortar and pestle, pound the mint leaves and sea salt to a smooth paste. Stir in the coconut yogurt and apple. If the yogurt is too thick, thin with a little water. Season with pepper to taste.

7 Serve the samosas warm, accompanied by the raita and with lemon wedges for squeezing over.

Beet and za'atar dip with pita chips

PREP + COOK TIME 1 HOUR | SERVES 4 (MAKES 2½ CUPS)

With its characteristic jewel-like hue, beet can't help but be a vivid inclusion in any recipe.
Za'atar, a Middle Eastern spice blend, balances the sweetness of beets here with its own
characteristic balance of herby earthiness and citrusy tartness provided by sumac.

1⅓ lb (600g) red beets, trimmed

¼ cup (60ml) olive oil, divided, plus
extra 2 tsp to drizzle

2 (8-in/20cm) whole grain pita breads

1 tbsp pumpkin seeds

½ lemon

⅔ cup (100g) roasted unsalted cashews

¼ cup (70g) dairy-free yogurt

¾ tsp sumac

1½ tsp za'atar, divided

sea salt and freshly ground black pepper

1 Preheat the oven to 350°F (180°C).

2 Scrub the beets well. Cut into ½-in (1cm) cubes. Combine the beets and
1 tablespoon of the olive oil on a large baking tray; season with salt and
pepper to taste. Roast for 40 minutes; allow to cool.

3 Meanwhile, cut the pita breads into wedges. Arrange the bread on 2 large
baking sheets. Brush with the remaining olive oil, and season with sea
salt to taste. Bake for 10 minutes or until golden and crisp, turning over
halfway through the cooking time. Spread the pumpkin seeds over
a medium baking tray; toast for 5 minutes.

4 Remove the zest from the lemon using a zester. (If you don't have a zester,
thinly peel the zest from the lemon, avoiding the white pith. Cut the zest
into long, thin strips.) Squeeze 1 tablespoon lemon juice from the lemon.

5 Reserve ¼ cup of the roasted beets. Process the remaining beets in a
food processor until they form a smooth consistency. Add the cashews;
process until fine. Add the 1 tablespoon lemon juice, yogurt, sumac, and
1 teaspoon of the za'atar; pulse until combined. Season with salt and
pepper to taste.

6 Transfer the beet mixture to a bowl, then drizzle with the extra
2 teaspoons olive oil. Sprinkle with the remaining ½ teaspoon za'atar;
top with the reserved chopped beets, toasted pumpkin seeds, and
lemon zest. Serve the dip with the pita chips.

TIPS

- Make bagel chips from thinly cut bagels instead of
pita bread, if you'd like.
- Top the dip with pine nuts, chopped almonds, or
sunflower seeds instead of pumpkin seeds.
- Serve with crudités such as carrot or radish cut
into matchsticks.

Spiced white bean and Greek salad pitas

PREP + COOK TIME **20 MINUTES** | SERVES **4**

Use the recipe below to make your own tofu feta or buy a good-quality feta-style vegan cheese instead. Either way, this is a fantastic option for a portable lunch for work (see tips). Cannellini beans are an excellent source of fiber and protein, so it makes it a filling one too.

¼ cup (60ml) olive oil

⅓ cup (100g) finely chopped red onion

1 garlic clove, crushed

¼ tsp dried oregano leaves

2 tsp ground cumin

1 (15 oz/425g) can cannellini beans, drained, rinsed (see tips)

1 tbsp freshly squeezed lemon juice

1 tbsp chopped fresh flat-leaf parsley

4 (8-in/20cm) whole grain pita breads

⅓ cup (100g) vegan mayonnaise
(see Everyday Mayo on page 55 or use store-bought)

¼ cup (40g) pitted kalamata olives, halved

2 small cucumbers (120g), quartered lengthwise

8 golden cherry tomatoes, halved

1 cup (250g) tofu feta (see right or use store-bought)

salt and freshly ground black pepper

1 lemon, cut into wedges, to serve

1 Heat the olive oil in a large skillet over medium heat; cook the onion, stirring, for 3 minutes or until softened. Increase the heat to high. Add the garlic, oregano, cumin, and cannellini beans; cook, stirring, for 2 minutes or until lightly browned. Add the lemon juice and parsley; season with salt and pepper to taste.

2 Meanwhile, warm the pita breads following the packet directions.

3 Spread the pita breads with the vegan mayonnaise. Combine the olives, cucumbers, tomatoes, and tofu feta in a medium bowl. Spoon into the pockets with the warm bean mixture.

4 Serve the pita breads with lemon wedges for squeezing over.

tofu feta You will need to start this recipe a day ahead to allow time for overnight refrigeration. Whisk together ½ cup (125ml) soy milk, ⅓ cup (80ml) rice wine vinegar, 1 tablespoon lemon juice, 1 teaspoon dried oregano, 1 crushed garlic clove, and 2 teaspoons salt in a large, shallow glass or ceramic dish. Add 13 oz (375g) extra-firm tofu, cubed; turn to coat. Cover with plastic wrap; refrigerate overnight. Drain the "feta" and use right away, or pat dry and place in a container with 1 teaspoon black peppercorns, 1 tablespoon chopped rosemary, 2 tablespoons torn pitted kalamata olives, and about 2 cups (500ml) olive oil or enough oil to cover; seal. The marinated tofu feta will keep in the fridge for up to 2 weeks (makes about ¾ lb or 375g). Alternatively, use one of the variations below.

chili tofu feta Make the tofu feta as above. Pat dry and put in the container. Omit the black peppercorns, rosemary, and olives. Combine the olive oil with 1 thinly sliced fresh long red chile, 1 thinly sliced shallot, and 2 sprigs of thyme.

lemon tofu feta Make the tofu feta as above. Pat dry and put in the container. Omit the rosemary and olives. Combine the olive oil and black peppercorns with 3 bay leaves and 3 wide strips of lemon zest.

TIPS

- Save the drained liquid from the canned cannellini beans, called aquafaba, to use in the Everyday Mayo (page 55) or meringues (page 158). You can store it in the fridge for 2 days or freeze for up to 3 months.
- To transport, pack the pita pockets, mayonnaise, and salad separately; assemble just before serving.

Satay tofu and roast butternut squash wraps

PREP + COOK TIME **40 MINUTES** | SERVES **4–6**

When you are looking for something filling, nutritious, and flavor-filled for lunch, these wraps fit the bill—particularly if you are taking them to work or going on a picnic. To transport, wrap the finished rolls first in parchment paper, then firmly in plastic wrap.

¼ cup (60ml) canned coconut milk

1 tbsp crunchy natural peanut butter

1 tsp tamari

1 lb (450g) satay-marinated tofu, cut into 1-in- (2.5cm) thick rectangles

1 lb (450g) butternut squash, peeled, cut into ½-in- (1.25cm) thick slices

1 tbsp olive oil

4 (8-in/20cm) spinach and herb wraps (see tips)

1 head romaine, trimmed, whole or shredded

1 cup (80g) finely shredded red cabbage

1 cup (100g) snow peas, trimmed, thinly sliced

1 red bell pepper (150g), thinly sliced

1 yellow bell pepper (150g), thinly sliced

1 red beet (150g), peeled, cut into matchsticks

1 avocado (250g)

sprigs of cilantro and mint leaves (optional)

salt and freshly ground black pepper

1 Preheat the oven to 400°F (200°C). Line 2 baking sheets with parchment paper.

2 Combine the coconut milk, peanut butter, and tamari in a medium bowl. Dip the tofu pieces in the mixture to coat; place on one of the lined trays.

3 Arrange the squash on the remaining tray; toss with olive oil and season with salt and pepper to taste. Roast the tofu and butternut squash for 20 minutes, turning halfway through the cooking time, or until golden.

4 Place the wraps on a clean work surface. Divide the lettuce, cabbage, snow peas, peppers, beet, tofu, and squash among the wraps. Thinly slice the avocado and divide evenly among the wraps. Top with a few sprigs of cilantro and mint leaves, if you'd like. Roll up tightly; cut in half.

TIPS

- The wraps used here are spinach and herb (it's why they're green!), but you can use other wraps such as sweet potato wraps or whole grain instead.
- Make these into rice paper rolls by substituting rice paper wrappers for the bread wraps. Cut the squash and tofu into smaller pieces, and use at least 8 rounds of rice paper.
- The tofu and butternut squash can be eaten warm if using immediately; if you are making these wraps to go, allow to cool before placing inside the wraps.

Miso peanut bowl with shredded vegetables

PREP + COOK TIME **20 MINUTES** | SERVES **4**

Shiro miso, also known as white miso, is golden in color. Lighter and mellower than other types, it has a more subtle umami flavor and a nutty sweetness, making it ideal for the dressing. For a more substantial meal, add sliced teriyaki-flavored or plain tofu.

1 fennel bulb (130g) (see tips)

1 cup (80g) finely shredded red cabbage

1 cup (80g) finely shredded green cabbage

1 large beet (150g), peeled, cut into matchsticks

1 lb (450g) baby carrots, trimmed, peeled into ribbons

$^1/_3$ cup (45g) finely chopped roasted unsalted peanuts

$^1/_2$ cup (10g) loosely packed mint leaves

1 lime (90g), cut into wedges

miso peanut dressing

$^1/_2$ cup (140g) crunchy natural peanut butter

$^1/_4$ cup (70g) white miso paste (shiro miso)

2 tbsp coconut sugar

$^1/_2$ tsp finely grated lime zest

1 fresh small red chile, finely chopped (see tips)

$^1/_3$ cup (80ml) lime juice

1 Make the miso peanut dressing. Blend or process the ingredients with $^1/_2$ cup (125ml) water until combined.

2 Thinly slice the fennel bulb and stems (see tips).

3 Divide the fennel, red and green cabbage, beets, and carrots among 4 serving bowls; top with the peanuts and mint. Serve with the miso peanut dressing and lime wedges for squeezing over.

TIPS

- Use a mandoline for the vegetables for best results. Toss the fennel in lime juice to prevent it from browning if not serving immediately.
- Seed the chile if you prefer less heat.
- When traveling, store the dressing and the salad ingredients separately; combine when serving.

Broccoli arancini with arugula and almond pesto

PREP + COOK TIME **50 MINUTES + COOLING** | SERVES **4 (MAKES 16)**

Arancini are a staple of Sicilian cuisine, and this vegan-suitable rendition bears all the classic hallmarks of the traditional dish. The crisp coating encases zesty risotto-style rice, and broccoli brings its own benefits, including a hefty dose of antioxidants such as vitamin C.

3 cups (750ml) vegetable stock

2 tbsp olive oil

1 leek (350g), finely chopped

1 garlic clove, crushed

1 cup (200g) arborio rice

1 cup (250ml) dry white wine

$1/3$ lb (150g) broccoli, cut into small florets

2 tsp finely grated lemon zest

$1^{1}/_{2}$ cups (110g) packaged gluten-free bread crumbs (see tips)

grape-seed oil, for deep-frying

salt and freshly ground black pepper

arugula and almond pesto

5 cups (100g) arugula, coarsely chopped

$1/_{2}$ cup (80g) roasted blanched almonds, coarsely chopped

2 tbsp nutritional yeast flakes

$1/_{2}$ cup (125ml) olive oil

TIPS

- Gluten-free bread crumbs are available at most grocery stores. As with other bread crumbs, always check the label first for any dairy products.
- This recipe is ideal with leftover risotto, or make the risotto a day before rolling the balls. Store the pesto in a small airtight container, with plastic wrap directly on the surface, in the fridge.
- Serve with a green leaf or tomato salad and lemon wedges for squeezing over.

1 Bring the vegetable stock to a boil in a large saucepan. Reduce the heat; simmer, covered.

2 Meanwhile, heat the olive oil in a medium saucepan over medium heat; cook the leek and garlic, stirring, for 2 minutes or until the leek is soft. Reduce the heat to low. Add the rice; stir to coat the grains in the oil mixture. Add the wine; cook, stirring, for 2 minutes or until the wine is absorbed.

3 Stir in ½ cup (125ml) of the hot stock; cook, stirring, over low heat until the liquid is absorbed. Continue adding stock in $^{1}/_{2}$-cup (125ml) batches, stirring until the liquid is absorbed after each addition. The total cooking time should be about 20 minutes or until the rice is just tender, with the broccoli being added during the last 10 minutes of cooking. Stir in the lemon zest; season with salt and pepper to taste. Spread the rice mixture over a large baking tray; allow to cool for 15 minutes.

4 With wet hands, roll $^{1}/_{4}$ cup of the rice mixture into a ball; continue until all the rice is used. Toss the balls in the bread crumbs to coat; place on a tray. Refrigerate for 30 minutes.

5 Meanwhile, make the arugula and almond pesto. Process the ingredients in a small food processor until almost smooth. Transfer to a small bowl; season with salt and pepper to taste.

6 Fill a large saucepan one-third full with grape-seed oil; heat to 350°F (180°C) or until a cube of bread turns golden in 15 seconds. Deep-fry the balls in batches for 2 minutes, turning occasionally, until lightly browned and heated through. Drain on paper towels.

7 Serve the arancini with the arugula and almond pesto.

Wasabi edamame hummus pack

PREP + COOK TIME **30 MINUTES** | SERVES **4**

This is a brilliant way to whip up a grazing board that looks impressive without too much effort. Edamame beans are high in protein, iron, and calcium, while the wasabi paste adds a kick to the hummus. The pairing of edamame and wasabi is a popular one in Japanese cuisine.

1 cup (200g) shelled edamame beans, thawed if frozen

1 (15 oz/425g) can chickpeas, drained, rinsed

$^1/_4$ cup (60ml) lime juice

2 tbsp tahini

$1^1/_2$ tsp wasabi paste

1 small garlic clove, crushed

salt and freshly ground black pepper

olive oil, to drizzle

black sesame seeds, to serve (optional)

sesame crisps

12 (5-in/13cm) frozen spring roll or rice paper wrappers (see tips)

vegetable oil cooking spray

2 tsp black sesame seeds

1 tsp sea salt flakes

quick pickled vegetables

$^3/_4$ cup (180ml) rice wine vinegar

$^1/_2$ cup (125ml) pure maple syrup

$^1/_4$ cup (60ml) soy sauce

6 radishes (210g), quartered

6 small cucumbers (180g), quartered lengthwise

1 First, make the sesame crisps and quick pickled vegetables. Preheat the oven to 350°F (180°C). Line 2 oven trays with parchment paper. Spray half of the spring roll wrappers with vegetable oil cooking spray. Top each with a second wrapper; cut in half to make 12 rectangles. Place the rectangles on the prepared trays; spray with vegetable oil, then sprinkle with the sesame seeds and sea salt. Bake for 10 minutes or until golden. Allow to cool. Break into pieces for dipping.

2 To make the quick pickled vegetables, stir together the rice wine vinegar, maple syrup, and soy sauce in a small saucepan until almost simmering. Put the radishes and cucumbers in a medium heatproof bowl; pour the vinegar mixture over the vegetables. Cover; refrigerate for 20 minutes.

3 Reserve 1 tablespoon of the edamame for serving. Put the remaining edamame in a food processor with the chickpeas, lime juice, tahini, wasabi paste, garlic, and $^1/_4$ cup (60ml) water; process until smooth. Season with salt and pepper to taste.

4 Spoon the dip into a serving bowl; top with the reserved edamame beans. Sprinkle over some black sesame seeds and drizzle with a little olive oil, if you'd like. Place the dip on a platter with the sesame crisps and pickled vegetables.

TIPS

• You will find spring roll wrappers in the freezer section of the store. Thaw before using.

• The quick pickled vegetables are best made on the day of serving.

King Kong cookies

PREP + COOK TIME **35 MINUTES** | MAKES **20**

Just as their namesake suggests, these are monster-sized cookies to tide you over until your next big meal. Whether it's for a morning snack or a treat in your lunchbox just in case, with their satisfying crunch and blend of sweet and salty, they will not disappoint.

2 bananas (400g unpeeled)

2$^1/_2$ cups (225g) rolled oats

1 cup (75g) shredded coconut

$^1/_2$ cup (70g) roasted salted peanuts, coarsely chopped

$^1/_3$ cup (35g) cacao powder, sifted

$^1/_2$ cup (125ml) pure maple syrup

$^1/_4$ cup (60ml) olive oil

8 soft fresh dates (160g), pitted, finely chopped

$^1/_2$ tsp salt

$^1/_4$ cup (35g) cacao nibs (see tips)

1 Preheat the oven to 350°F (180°C). Line 2 baking sheets with parchment paper.

2 Mash the bananas in a large bowl until smooth; you will need $^3/_4$ cup (180g) mashed banana. Add the remaining ingredients, except for the cacao nibs, to the bowl. Using clean hands, mix until well combined.

3 Using damp hands, roll heaped tablespoons of the mixture into balls. Place on the prepared trays. Flatten slightly to 3-inch (7.5cm) rounds (the cookies will not spread when cooking). Sprinkle with the cacao nibs.

4 Bake the cookies for 20 minutes or until golden brown on the outside. Allow to cool on the trays.

TIPS

• Cacao nibs are fermented crushed dried cacao beans. When they are ground to a liquor, they become the starting point for making chocolate, before sugar and milk are added. They are available at large grocery stores and health food shops.

• Store the cookies in an airtight container at room temperature for up to 3 days or freeze in airtight bags for up to 1 month.

BIG PLATES

Weeknight suppers, weekend lunches, cozy nights in, dinner with family, or entertaining friends—from hearty mains to tempting sides, these meals are made for savoring.

Spicy not-kotsu ramen

PREP + COOK TIME **15 MINUTES + STANDING** | SERVES **4**

This is our playful and flavor-packed vegan take on tonkotsu ramen, traditionally a pork-based dish with origins in Fukuoka, Japan. Here, shiitake mushrooms impart their characteristic rich umami taste to the broth and up the protein intake alongside the tofu.

¼ cup (60ml) olive oil

2 tsp finely grated fresh ginger

6 garlic cloves, crushed

4 green onions, thinly sliced, green tips shredded and reserved for garnish

2 tbsp chile oil

2 tbsp white miso paste (shiro miso) (see tips)

⅓ cup (80ml) mirin

⅓ cup (80ml) soy sauce

2 cups (500ml) soy milk

2 ears of corn (500g), husks and silk removed

4 baby bok choy (240g), halved

9.5 oz (270g) dried ramen noodles

7 oz (200g) silken tofu, cubed

2 tbsp sesame seeds, toasted, crushed (see tips)

dashi

0.75 oz (25g) dried shiitake mushrooms

1.5 oz (40g) dried kombu

1 First, make the dashi. Put the shiitake mushrooms and dried kombu in a large saucepan with 6 cups (1.5 liters) cold tap water; slowly bring to a boil over low heat. Remove from the heat; allow to stand for 30 minutes for the flavors to infuse. Strain the liquid through a fine mesh strainer into a large bowl. Slice the mushrooms, reserving in a small bowl; discard the kombu.

2 Heat the olive oil in a large saucepan over medium heat; cook the ginger, garlic, and sliced green onions for 4 minutes or until softened. Add the chile oil and miso; cook, stirring, for 1 minute. Add the mirin and soy sauce; bring to the boil.

3 Reduce the heat to medium. Add the reserved dashi and the soy milk; cook for 5 minutes or until just below boiling point. Strain through a fine mesh strainer; discard the solids. Stir in the reserved sliced mushrooms.

4 Meanwhile, bring a large saucepan of water to a boil. Cook the corn for 10 minutes or until tender; remove with tongs. Add the bok choy to the water; cook for 2 minutes or until tender, then remove with tongs. Add the noodles to the same water; cook for 5 minutes or until tender. Drain. Cut the kernels from the corn cobs.

5 Divide the noodles and bok choy evenly among 4 serving bowls. Pour over the hot broth. Top with the corn kernels, shredded green onion, and tofu. Serve sprinkled with the sesame seeds.

TIPS

• Always check the ingredients listed on miso pastes. Some brands contain bonito (tuna) extract, which is unsuitable for vegans.

• To toast the sesame seeds, stir continuously in a small skillet over medium heat until golden. Crush using a mortar and pestle.

Beet Wellington

PREP + COOK TIME **3 HOURS 20 MINUTES** | SERVES **6**

It is important to buy beets that are equal in size for this recipe so that the pastry encases them snugly and your Wellington looks its most elegant.

2½ lb (1.2kg) red beets, scrubbed (about 6 large) (see tips)

¼ cup (60ml) olive oil, divided

1 tbsp sherry vinegar

1 tbsp fresh thyme leaves, divided

4 shallots, finely chopped

2 cups (200g) walnuts, toasted, coarsely chopped

2 tbsp flaxseed meal

1 tsp ground nutmeg

⅓ cup (80ml) white wine

8 cups (240g) baby spinach leaves

3 sheets of frozen puff pastry

1 tbsp almond milk

1 tbsp vegan sugar

salt and freshly ground black pepper

TIPS

• Beet greens are edible. If you buy beets with the leaves still attached, trim and wash the young leaves. Blanch in a saucepan of boiling water until just wilted; drain. Toss the leaves with a little olive oil; season with salt and freshly ground black pepper. Serve alongside the beet Wellington.

• Serve with mashed potatoes and a horseradish cream; for horseradish cream, combine 1 teaspoon prepared horseradish with ⅓ cup (80ml) vegan mayonnaise or dairy-free yogurt.

1 Preheat the oven to 400°F (200°C). Line a 9 x 9-inch (23 x 23cm) roasting dish and a large baking sheet with parchment paper.

2 Put the beets in the prepared roasting dish. Drizzle with 1 tablespoon of the olive oil and the vinegar. Sprinkle with half of the thyme leaves; season generously with salt and pepper. Cover the tin with parchment paper and then foil; seal well. Roast the beets for 1 hour 20 minutes or until cooked through. Allow to cool; peel, then trim the ends.

3 Meanwhile, heat the remaining olive oil in a small skillet over medium heat; cook the shallots for 10 minutes. Add the walnuts, flaxseed meal, nutmeg, and remaining thyme. Stir in the wine and ¼ cup (60ml) water; cook for 2 minutes. Season with salt and pepper to taste. Cool.

4 Blanch the spinach in salted boiling water for 20 seconds; drain, then refresh in iced water. Drain again, squeezing out as much water as you can. Set aside.

5 Cut one of the pastry sheets in half, then join each half to a separate whole pastry sheet; press along the edges to seal. Next, join the 2 extended pieces of pastry to each other by joining on a long side to form a roughly 14 x 18-inch (36cm x 46cm) rectangle of pastry.

6 Spread the cooled walnut mixture in the middle of the pastry, leaving a 3-inch (8cm) border on the long sides and a 1½-inch (4cm) border on the short sides. Press to compact the mixture, then top with the reserved spinach, unraveling it slightly so that it sits flat. Place the beets upright on top, arranging them in a line next to each other. Trim away any excess pastry if needed, then roll the pastry over the beets to enclose the filling. Tuck the ends under, and place on the lined large baking sheet.

7 Combine the almond milk and sugar, and brush the pastry generously with the mixture. Using a sharp knife, score the top; sprinkle with pepper. Bake for 40 minutes, rotating the tray halfway through the cooking time. Serve the beet Wellington in slices.

Carrot and millet patties with sunflower slaw

PREP + COOK TIME **45 MINUTES** | SERVES **2**

Millet, a small, nutrient-dense seed, is packed with fiber, protein, B vitamins, and minerals—
as are sunflower seeds. Serve with a minty mayonnaise on the side, if you'd like.

1 cup (250ml) vegetable stock

1/2 cup (100g) millet

1 shallot, finely chopped

1/3 cup (50g) sun-dried tomatoes, finely chopped

1 carrot (120g), finely grated

1 tbsp tomato paste

1 tbsp freshly squeezed lemon juice

salt and freshly ground black pepper

lemon wedges, to serve

sunflower slaw

2 tbsp freshly squeezed lemon juice

1/4 cup (60ml) olive oil

2 tsp Dijon mustard

2 cups (160g) finely shredded green cabbage

1 cup (80g) finely shredded red cabbage

1/2 cup (10g) mint leaves

1/4 cup (40g) sunflower seeds, divided

1 Preheat the oven to 400°F (200°C). Line a baking sheet with parchment paper.

2 Bring the vegetable stock to a boil in a small saucepan. Reduce the heat to low; partially cover with a lid.

3 Stir the millet in a medium saucepan over medium heat for 3 minutes or until fragrant and toasted. Add the hot stock to the millet; stir well. Bring to a boil. Reduce the heat to low; cook the millet, covered, for 15 minutes or until the liquid is absorbed.

4 Transfer the millet to a food processor. Add the shallot, sun-dried tomatoes, carrot, tomato paste, and lemon juice. Season with salt and pepper to taste. Pulse until the mixture comes together but still has some texture.

5 Shape 1/4 cup portions of the millet mixture into 4 (3-inch/8cm) patties; place on the lined sheet. Bake for 20 minutes or until golden and crisp.

6 To make the sunflower slaw, blend the lemon juice, olive oil, and Dijon mustard in a blender until smooth. Season with salt and pepper to taste. Put the green and red cabbage, mint, and 2 tablespoons of the sunflower seeds in a medium bowl with the dressing; toss well to combine. Sprinkle with the remaining sunflower seeds.

7 Serve the patties with the sunflower slaw, with lemon wedges for squeezing over and fresh mint mayonnaise (see tips), if you'd like.

TIPS

▪ You can make the dressing, shred the cabbage, and shape the patties (or even bake them) a day ahead. Store each ingredient separately in the fridge. Reheat the patties before serving.

▪ Serve with vegan mayonnaise (see Everyday Mayo, page 55) blended with 2 tablespoons coarsely chopped mint leaves and 2 teaspoons lemon juice.

Mushroom, spinach, and walnut pasta

PREP + COOK TIME **20 MINUTES** | SERVES **2**

Spelt, used here for the pasta, is an ancient grain with similarities to wheat. Unlike
all-purpose flour, which is refined by removing the germ and the bran, the nutritious part
of the spelt grain remains when it's milled into whole grain flour.

⅓ cup (80ml) olive oil, divided

½ cup (50g) raw walnuts

5 oz (140g) dried spelt fusilli pasta (see tips)

5 oz (140g) enoki mushrooms (see tips)

2 garlic cloves, finely chopped

1 long red chile, seeded, finely chopped

2 tsp apple cider vinegar

9 oz (280g) baby spinach leaves, washed

salt and freshly ground black pepper

1 Heat 1 tablespoon of the olive oil in a small skillet over medium heat;
cook the walnuts, stirring continuously, for 5 minutes or until golden
and toasted. Remove from the pan; allow to cool. Coarsely chop the nuts.
Set aside.

2 Cook the pasta in a large saucepan of boiling salted water for 12 minutes
or until almost tender. Drain. Return the pasta to the pan off the heat;
cover and keep warm until needed.

3 Meanwhile, heat the remaining olive oil in a medium saucepan over
medium-high heat; cook the mushrooms for 2 minutes or until tender
and golden. Add the garlic and chile; cook, stirring, for 1 minute or until
fragrant. Add the vinegar; cook for 1 minute. Add the spinach and toasted
walnuts; cook for 1 minute or until the spinach is lightly wilted. Season
with salt and pepper to taste.

4 Add the mushroom-spinach mixture to the pasta; toss well to coat
the pasta.

TIPS

- You can use any shaped spelt pasta for this recipe.
- You can find enoki mushrooms at your favorite
Asian grocery store. You can use shiitake or oyster
mushrooms or a combination if you'd prefer.

Sweet and spicy tofu noodles

PREP + COOK TIME **30 MINUTES** | SERVES **2**

Fresh ginger and chile add a kick to this simple stir-fry, while crispy fried shallots
finish everything off with a crunch. You can also serve this dish topped with chile crisp,
chopped peanuts, and lime wedges.

7 oz (200g) dried rice stick noodles

8 oz (225g) firm tofu

1 tbsp peanut oil

1 garlic clove, crushed

1 tbsp finely chopped fresh ginger

8 oz (225g) fresh stir-fry vegetables

¼ cup (60ml) sweet chile sauce

2 tbsp sriracha

2 tsp tamari

1½ cups (50g) beansprouts, plus extra to serve

2 tbsp fried shallots (see tips)

⅓ cup (10g) loosely packed cilantro leaves

1 Put the noodles in a large heatproof bowl; pour in enough boiling water to cover. Allow to stand for 5 minutes or until the noodles soften. Drain.

2 Meanwhile, pat the tofu dry with paper towels to remove as much moisture as possible. Cut the tofu into 1-inch (2.5cm) cubes.

3 Heat the peanut oil in a wok or large skillet over medium-high heat. Add the tofu; cook for 1 minute on each side or until golden. Remove with a slotted spoon. Add the garlic, ginger, and stir-fry vegetables to the wok; cook for 1 minute or until the vegetables are just starting to soften.

4 Add the drained noodles, sweet chile sauce, sriracha, tamari, and the beansprouts; stir-fry gently to prevent the noodles breaking up, until just combined and heated through.

5 Divide the mixture between 2 serving bowls. Top with the tofu, extra beansprouts, fried shallots, and cilantro.

TIPS

- To make your own stir-fry mix, combine broccoli florets, sugar snap peas, and red bell pepper strips.
- Fried shallots are a popular garnish in Southeast Asian cooking and are readily available from Asian grocers. Make sure to seek out a good-quality brand, or make your own, if you'd like.

Lunch bowls

These nutritious bowls are a fast answer to what to do for lunch or supper. Recipe quantities can easily be halved or doubled. Even experiment with different grains and vegetables.

Rainbow avocado bowl

PREP TIME 10 MINUTES | SERVES 2

In a small bowl, stir 1 tablespoon tahini, 1$\frac{1}{2}$ tablespoons water, 1 tablespoon lemon juice, and 2 teaspoons olive oil until combined. Set aside. Halve and pit 1 large avocado (320g), and place the halves cut-side up on a plate. Fill each half with $\frac{1}{2}$ small carrot (25g), julienned or grated, $\frac{1}{2}$ small red beet (50g), julienned or grated, 2 tablespoons kimchi, and 1 tablespoon pea shoots, if you'd like. Season with salt and freshly ground black pepper to taste. Drizzle with the lemon tahini dressing.

Mixed-grain bowl

PREP + COOK TIME 20 MINUTES | SERVES 2

In a food processor, process 2 tablespoons tahini, $\frac{1}{4}$ cup (8g) basil, 3 teaspoons white wine vinegar, and $\frac{1}{2}$ cup (125ml) water until smooth. Season with salt and freshly ground black pepper. Set aside. Heat 2 tablespoons olive oil in a large skillet over medium-high heat. Add 1 crushed garlic clove; cook for 30 seconds. Add 1 cup (250g) instant brown rice and quinoa; cook, stirring, for 5 minutes until starting to crisp. Transfer to a bowl to keep warm. Add 1 tablespoon olive oil to the same pan; cook 10 oz (300g) halved Brussels sprouts, turning occasionally, for 5 minutes or until tender and charred. Transfer to a plate; keep warm. Add another 1 tablespoon olive oil to the pan. Cook 2 cups Tuscan kale leaves, turning, for 2 minutes or until just starting to wilt. Transfer to a plate; keep warm. Divide the rice mixture between 2 bowls; top with the Brussels sprouts, kale, 1 sliced avocado (250g), $\frac{1}{4}$ cup (50g) pumpkin seeds, the tahini dressing, and 1 tablespoon basil leaves.

Miso cashew bowl

PREP + COOK TIME 20 MINUTES + 4 HOURS' STANDING | SERVES 4

Put 1 cup (150g) raw cashews in a small bowl; cover with water. Allow to stand, covered, for 4 hours; drain. In a high-powered blender, blend with 2 tablespoons white miso paste, 2 tablespoons coconut sugar, $\frac{1}{2}$ teaspoon finely grated lime zest, 1 small chopped red chile, $\frac{1}{3}$ cup (80ml) lime juice, and $\frac{1}{2}$ cup (125ml) water until smooth. Thinly slice 1 baby fennel bulb (130g); toss in a little lime juice. Divide the fennel, 2 cups (160g) finely shredded red cabbage, 1 lb (450g) baby carrots, peeled into ribbons, and 1 beet (150g), cut into matchsticks, among 4 bowls. Top with $\frac{1}{3}$ cup (45g) finely chopped raw cashews and $\frac{1}{2}$ cup (10g) mint leaves. Serve with the miso cashew dressing, sliced red chile, and lime wedges.

Spicy soba noodle bowl

PREP + COOK TIME 20 MINUTES | SERVES 2

Cut 1 green onion into 2-inch (5cm) lengths, then into long strips; put in a bowl of iced water to curl. Combine $\frac{1}{2}$ teaspoon red pepper flakes, 2 crushed small garlic cloves, 2 tablespoons tamari, 2 tablespoons Chinese black vinegar, 1 tablespoon sesame oil, and 2 thinly sliced green onions in a small bowl. Bring a saucepan of salted water to a boil over high heat. Cook 1 lb (450g) Swiss chard for 1 minute until just tender. Remove with tongs; place on a plate. Drizzle with 1 tablespoon sesame oil. Add 6 oz (180g) dried green tea soba noodles to the boiling water; cook for 3 minutes. Add 1 cup (250g) thawed frozen shelled edamame; cook for 1 minute to heat. Drain; return to the pan. Gently toss in the chile-garlic sauce. Serve topped with the green onion curls and toasted sesame seeds.

Coconut and split pea curry

PREP + COOK TIME **1 HOUR 20 MINUTES** | SERVES **4**

Split peas are a nutrient-dense legume containing fiber, iron, protein, minerals, and vitamins
A and B to support a good immune system and eyesight, assist in red blood cell production,
and help to convert energy from the foods we eat. Serve the curry with brown rice, if desired.

1 cup (200g) yellow split peas

1¹/₂ cups (600g) squash, such as kabocha, peeled,
seeded, and cut into 1-in (2.5cm) cubes

¹/₄ cup (60ml) olive oil, divided

³/₄ cup (200g) diced onion

1 tsp finely grated fresh ginger

4 garlic cloves, crushed

1 tbsp garam masala

4 cups (1 liter) vegetable stock

1 cup (250ml) canned coconut cream

¹/₂ lb (225g) green beans, trimmed

1 tbsp freshly squeezed lime juice

salt and freshly ground black pepper

to serve

cilantro leaves

mint leaves

nigella seeds

lime wedges

1 Put the split peas in a large heatproof bowl with enough boiling water
to cover. Allow to stand until needed.

2 Preheat the oven to 425°F (220°C). Line a baking sheet with
parchment paper.

3 Arrange the squash in a single layer on the baking sheet; drizzle with
a little of the olive oil. Season with salt and pepper to taste. Roast for
25 minutes or until golden.

4 Meanwhile, heat the remaining olive oil in a large saucepan over medium
heat. Cook the onion for 4 minutes or until softened. Add the ginger and
garlic; cook for 1 minute. Stir in the garam masala; cook for a further
minute or until fragrant.

5 Add the drained split peas and vegetable stock to the saucepan. Increase
the heat to high; cook, stirring frequently, for 30 minutes or until the
split peas are soft and the curry is thick.

6 Reduce the heat to medium. Add the coconut cream, green beans, and
roasted squash; stir to combine. Simmer for 2 minutes or until the beans
are just tender. Stir in the lime juice; season with salt and pepper.

7 Serve the curry topped with cilantro, mint, nigella seeds, and lime
wedges for squeezing over. Or keep it simple and serve without
the toppings, if you'd like.

Mushroom "steak" sandwich

PREP + COOK TIME **20 MINUTES** | SERVES **2**

Mushrooms' umami flavor and dense, meaty texture make them ideal for this sandwich.
This lazy recipe is easy on the pocket book, too, with only a few fresh ingredients needed.

$^1/_4$ cup (60ml) olive oil

$^3/_4$ cup (200g) thinly sliced onion

1 large green bell pepper (350g), thinly sliced

13 oz (375g) portabella mushrooms, sliced

2 garlic cloves, crushed

2 tbsp smoky barbecue sauce

$^1/_3$ cup (80ml) vegan beef-like stock (see tips)

2 slices of vegan cheddar (36g), halved

2 long seeded bread rolls (100g), split in half

2 tbsp yellow mustard

salt and freshly ground black pepper

fresh or pickled sliced jalapeños,
to serve (optional)

1 Heat the olive oil in a large non-stick skillet over high heat; cook the onion and green pepper for 4 minutes or until softened. Add the mushrooms; cook, stirring, for 5 minutes or until golden. Add the garlic; stir for 1 minute. Add the barbecue sauce and vegan stock; cook for 2 minutes or until thickened. Season with salt and pepper to taste.

2 Place the vegan cheddar in the bread rolls; spoon the hot mushroom mixture on top. Drizzle with the mustard; top with sliced jalapeños, if you'd like.

TIPS

- Mushrooms have a low caloric density and contain an important mix of minerals and vitamins. They are also one of the leading plant-based sources of selenium, an antioxidant that assists in warding off chronic diseases.

- There is an assortment of vegan stocks available that mimic chicken and beef flavors; these are labeled beef- or chicken-"like" and contain no animal products.

Bliss and chips with smashed peas

PREP + COOK TIME **1 HOUR + STANDING + REFRIGERATION** | SERVES **4**

Traditional fish and chips are often accompanied by classic English mushy peas. In this vegan version, battered eggplant is a delicious stand in for the crispy fish, and these updated, fresh smashed peas balance the dish with a nod to tradition.

1 lb (450g) Japanese eggplant

1 tbsp fine sea salt

4 nori sheets (10g), halved

1½ cups (200g) all-purpose flour, divided

1½ cups (375ml) pale ale

1½ lbs (750g) Russet potatoes, scrubbed (unpeeled)

2 tbsp olive oil

vegetable oil, for frying

salt and freshly ground black pepper

1 large lemon (200g), cut into wedges to serve

tartar sauce

4 cornichons, finely chopped

1 green onion, finely chopped

1 cup (300g) vegan mayonnaise
(use Everyday Mayo on page 55 or use store-bought)

2 tbsp baby capers

smashed peas

2 cups (240g) frozen green peas

¼ cup (60g) vegan margarine spread

4 sprigs of mint

1 tbsp freshly squeezed lemon juice

1 Preheat the oven to 400°F (200°C). Line 2 baking sheets with parchment paper.

2 Halve the eggplants lengthwise; place in a colander. Sprinkle with salt; allow to stand for 30 minutes. Rinse the eggplant under cold water. Gently squeeze out any excess water.

3 Wrap each eggplant half in a piece of nori (the moisture will help the nori stick to the eggplant). Refrigerate for 15 minutes.

4 Make the tartar sauce. Combine all of the ingredients in a small bowl.

5 Next, make the smashed peas. Cook the green peas, margarine, and mint in a small saucepan over medium heat for 6 minutes or until tender. Discard the mint. Using a hand-held blender, pulse the peas, leaving some whole. Season with salt and pepper to taste; stir in the lemon juice.

6 Put 1¼ cups (160g) of the flour in a bowl; season with salt and pepper. Gradually whisk in the beer to make a smooth batter. Allow to stand at room temperature for 30 minutes.

7 Cut the unpeeled potatoes into chunky French fries. Place the potato pieces on the prepared baking sheets; drizzle with the olive oil, then season with salt and pepper to taste. Bake for 30 minutes or until golden and crisp.

8 Meanwhile, fill a large saucepan or deep-fryer one-third full with vegetable oil; heat to 350°F (180°C) or until a cube of bread turns golden in 8 seconds. Dust the eggplant halves in the remaining ¼ cup (40g) flour. Dip into the batter, allowing any excess to drain off. Fry in two batches for 3 minutes each or until golden, turning halfway through the cooking time. Drain on a wire rack lined with paper towels.

9 Serve the fried eggplant with the French fries, smashed peas, tartar sauce, and lemon wedges.

Pulled jackfruit bao buns

PREP + COOK TIME **40 MINUTES** | SERVES **4**

A large tropical fruit with a meaty texture and neutral taste, jackfruit readily absorbs other flavors and can be used in sweet and savory dishes. It is also a good source of protein, fiber, and antioxidants, as well as vitamins and minerals such as vitamin C and manganese.

1 (20 oz/565g) can young green jackfruit in brine (see tips), drained, rinsed

1/2 cup (130g) hoisin sauce

2 tbsp pure maple syrup

2 tbsp tamari

1/4 tsp Chinese five-spice powder

1 small seedless European cucumber (5 oz/130g), thinly sliced

1 long red chile, thinly sliced

2 tbsp rice wine vinegar

8 frozen mini mantou or bao buns (180g) (see tips)

2 tbsp vegan mayonnaise (use Everyday Mayo on page 55 or use store-bought)

1 green onion, thinly sliced

1/3 cup (10g) cilantro leaves

1/3 cup (50g) roasted salted peanuts, finely chopped

salt and freshly ground black pepper

1 Cut the jackfruit into 1/2-inch (1.25cm) slices through the core. Combine the hoisin sauce, 1/4 cup (60ml) water, maple syrup, tamari, and five-spice powder in a medium saucepan over medium heat. Season with pepper to taste. Add the jackfruit; bring to a simmer. Cook for 20 minutes, stirring and breaking up the jackfruit with the back of a spoon, until the sauce has thickened and the mixture resembles pulled pork.

2 Meanwhile, combine the cucumber, chile, and rice wine vinegar in a medium bowl; season with salt and pepper to taste. Allow to stand for 5 minutes; drain.

3 Split the frozen buns three-quarters of the way through. Steam the buns, covered, in a bamboo steamer over a saucepan of simmering water for 5 minutes or until puffed up and heated through.

4 Spread the buns with the mayonnaise; fill with the jackfruit mixture, pickled cucumber mixture, green onion, cilantro, and peanuts.

TIPS

- Canned jackfruit can be found at Asian supermarkets and grocers. Ensure that you are buying jackfruit in brine, not syrup.
- You can use mantou buns or plain bao buns from your local Asian grocery store. You can also serve the pulled jackfruit in wraps or other soft slider buns, if you'd like.

Zucchini noodles with cashew pesto

PREP + COOK TIME 20 MINUTES + STANDING | SERVES 2

There are several methods you can use to make the zucchini noodles (see tips). You can also make your own Parmesan-style vegan cheese to go with them using the recipe below.

1⅓ lb (600g) large zucchini (about 4)

4 oz (125g) mixed heirloom cherry tomatoes, halved

¼ cup (7g) basil leaves

1 tbsp pine nuts

2 tbsp grated vegan Parmesan (see right or use store-bought)

salt and freshly ground black pepper

cashew pesto

⅔ cup (100g) raw cashews

1 cup (50g) firmly packed basil leaves

¼ cup (40g) pine nuts

2 tbsp freshly squeezed lemon juice

¼ cup (60ml) olive oil

2 tsp nutritional yeast flakes

1 garlic clove, crushed

1 To make the cashew pesto, put the cashews in a small bowl with enough cold water to cover. Allow to stand for 2 hours. Drain and rinse under cold water; drain well. In a food processor, process the drained cashews with the basil, pine nuts, lemon juice, olive oil, nutritional yeast flakes, and garlic until smooth. Season with salt and pepper to taste.

2 Using a spiralizer or julienne peeler, cut the zucchini into "noodles"; place in a large bowl.

3 Add the pesto and cherry tomatoes to the bowl; toss to combine. Top with the basil leaves, pine nuts, and vegan Parmesan. Season with salt and pepper to taste. Serve immediately.

vegan Parmesan In a food processor, process ¾ cup (115g) raw cashews, ⅓ cup (25g) nutritional yeast flakes, ¾ teaspoon sea salt flakes, and ¼ teaspoon garlic powder into a fine meal, similar in consistency to finely grated Parmesan cheese. Store in an airtight container in the fridge for up to 2 months. Use like regular Parmesan cheese.

TIPS

- Store any leftover pesto in an airtight container in the fridge for up to 1 week. Spread leftover pesto on toast or seeded crackers for a delicious snack.
- A spiralizer is a hand-cranked machine designed to cut vegetables into noodles or ribbons. A julienne peeler, or a wide-blade vegetable peeler with a serrated rather than straight blade, is another option. Both are available from kitchenware stores.
- If you don't have a spiralizer or julienne peeler, peel the zucchini into long ribbons, stack on top of one another, and cut into long, thin strips.

Coconut, tomato, and lentil soup

PREP + COOK TIME **30 MINUTES** | SERVES **4**

Save even more time and money by making a double batch of this comforting soup to freeze.
Its warmth will definitely be appreciated during cold weather. Blooming (or tempering)
the spices in the onion base brings out their essential oils and their full flavor and aroma.

1 tbsp coconut oil

¼ cup (80g) thinly sliced onion

2 tsp yellow mustard seeds

2 tsp curry powder

2 tbsp tomato paste

1 cup (200g) red lentils

4 cups (1 liter) vegetable stock

½ cup (125ml) canned coconut milk,
plus extra to drizzle

2 tomatoes (300g), coarsely chopped, divided

salt and freshly ground black pepper

sprigs of cilantro leaves
and lemon wedges, to serve

1 Heat the coconut oil in a medium saucepan over medium-high heat; cook the onion, stirring, for 3 minutes or until soft. Add the mustard seeds; stir for 4 minutes or until they start to pop. Add the curry powder; cook, stirring, for 1 minute. Add the tomato paste; cook, stirring, for a further 30 seconds.

2 Add the lentils, vegetable stock, and coconut milk; bring to a boil. Reduce the heat to low; simmer, covered, for 10 minutes, stirring occasionally, or until the lentils are tender. Stir in half of the tomatoes until just heated through. Season with salt and pepper to taste.

3 Ladle the soup into 4 serving bowls; drizzle with a little extra coconut milk, then top each serving with the remaining coarsely chopped tomato and a few cilantro leaves. Serve with lemon wedges.

TIPS

- Turn this soup into a curry by reducing the quantity of stock by 1 cup (250ml). You could also serve the soup topped with coarsely chopped smoked almonds or crushed popadams.
- The soup can be frozen at the end of step 2. Freeze in airtight containers for up to 1 month. Thaw and gently reheat.

Spaghetti with mushroom "meatballs"

PREP + COOK TIME **1 HOUR + REFRIGERATION** | SERVES **4**

These "meatballs" are powered by the incredibly satisfying and hearty taste of mushrooms.
Serve sprinkled with vegan Parmesan, if you'd like. (To make your own, see page 112.)

½ cup (120ml) olive oil, divided

¾ cup (200g) finely chopped onion

1⅓ lb (600g) cremini or button mushrooms, finely chopped

4 garlic cloves, crushed

2 tsp dried oregano

1 cup (100g) fresh bread crumbs

⅔ cup (60g) rolled oats

1 (15 oz/425g) can chickpeas, drained, rinsed

1 oz (28g) dried shiitake mushrooms, finely chopped or ground (see tip)

⅓ cup (10g) finely chopped flat-leaf parsley, divided

¼ cup (40g) all-purpose flour, divided

1 lb (450g) dried spaghetti

salt and freshly ground black pepper

marinara sauce

2 tbsp olive oil

¾ cup (200g) finely chopped onion

4 garlic cloves, crushed

1 tsp red pepper flakes (optional)

1 tsp dried oregano

½ cup (125ml) dry white wine

3 (15 oz/425g) cans crushed tomatoes

TIP

You can finely grind the dried shiitakes using a spice grinder or blender. They will create a fine powder that is a great way to build umami in a variety of vegan dishes.

1 Heat ¼ cup (60ml) olive oil in a large skillet over high heat; cook the onion for 4 minutes or until golden. Add the chopped button mushrooms and 2 tablespoons of the extra olive oil; cook for 10 minutes or until all liquid has evaporated and the mushrooms are golden.

2 Add the garlic and oregano; cook for a further minute. Remove from the heat; allow to cool for 5 minutes. In a food processor, pulse the mushroom mixture with the bread crumbs, rolled oats, chickpeas, shiitake mushrooms, and ¼ cup (7g) of the parsley until combined. Season with salt and pepper to taste. Pulse until the mixture is pasty.

3 Dust a large baking sheet with half of the flour. Using lightly damp hands, roll heaped tablespoons of the mixture into 24 balls; place them on the floured baking sheet. Sift the remaining flour over the meatballs. Refrigerate, uncovered, for 2 hours or until firm.

4 Meanwhile, make the marinara sauce. Heat the olive oil in a medium saucepan over medium heat; cook the onion for 4 minutes or until softened. Add the garlic, red pepper flakes (if using), and oregano; cook for a further minute or until fragrant. Increase the heat to high. Add the wine; cook for a minute or until evaporated. Add the tomatoes; bring to a boil. Reduce the heat to medium; simmer for 15 minutes or until slightly thickened. Season with salt and pepper to taste.

5 Heat the remaining 2 tablespoons of extra olive oil for the meatballs in a large, nonstick skillet over medium heat. Cook the meatballs in batches for 6 minutes, gently shaking the pan occasionally until evenly browned. Add the marinara sauce to the pan; toss very gently to combine and warm through, taking care not to break up the meatballs.

6 Meanwhile, cook the spaghetti in a large saucepan of boiling water for 12 minutes or until almost tender; drain.

7 Serve the spaghetti topped with the meatballs and sauce and sprinkled with the remaining parsley.

Tandoori tofu kebabs with mint yogurt sauce

PREP + COOK TIME **35 MINUTES** | MAKES **4**

This summery dish couldn't be easier to make and is ideal for an alfresco lunch or supper on a balmy evening. Remember to check the back label of the coconut yogurt for its entire list of ingredients—sugar is not always listed on the front.

olive oil cooking spray

1 lb (450g) firm tofu

1 red bell pepper (200g)

1 medium red onion (170g)

2 tomatoes (300g)

2 tbsp tandoori paste

$1/3$ cup (95g) unsweetened coconut yogurt (see tips)

1 tbsp small mint leaves

lime wedges, to serve

mint yogurt sauce

$1/2$ cup (140g) unsweetened coconut yogurt (see tips)

2 tbsp finely chopped mint leaves

$1/4$ cup (60ml) freshly squeezed lime juice

1 Preheat an oiled cast-iron grill pan or the grill. Soak 4 bamboo skewers in cold water to prevent them from scorching.

2 Using a paper towel, pat the tofu dry, then cut into 1 x 2-inch (2.5 x 5cm) pieces. Remove the seeds from the bell pepper. Cut the pepper and red onion each into eight 2-inch (5cm) pieces. Quarter the tomatoes.

3 In a medium bowl, combine the tandoori paste and coconut yogurt. Add the tofu; stir gently until evenly coated.

4 Thread the pepper, onion, tomatoes, and tofu onto the skewers, alternating the ingredients. Cook the kebabs for 5 minutes on each side or until the vegetables are tender and the tofu is golden.

5 To make the mint yogurt sauce, in a food processor, process the coconut yogurt, mint, and lime juice until smooth. (Alternatively, mix together the ingredients in a small bowl.)

6 Serve the tofu kebabs with the mint yogurt sauce, with the mint leaves sprinkled over the top and lime wedges for squeezing over.

TIPS

- These kebabs are a little on the spicy side; you may want to adjust the quantity of tandoori paste if you prefer a little less spice.
- The Homemade Coconut Yogurt on page 21 can be used for the mint yogurt sauce, but is unsuitable for coating the tofu because of the cooking.
- You can cook the kebabs in a preheated 425°F (220°C) oven for 30 minutes or until browned, turning the kebabs over halfway through the cooking time.

Vegan mac 'n' cheese

PREP + COOK TIME **50 MINUTES** | SERVES **4**

Macaroni and cheese is the ultimate comfort food, and now those going dairy-free can enjoy it, too, with this vegan macaroni and cheese. The "cheese" sauce part of the recipe can also be used to make a simple baked dish by layering with roasted eggplant.

1 lb (450g) dried macaroni

2 tbsp (30g) vegan margarine

$^1/_4$ cup (40g) all-purpose flour

1 tsp smoked paprika

$^1/_4$ tsp cayenne pepper

$^1/_4$ tsp garlic powder

3 cups (750ml) macadamia milk (see tips)

7 oz (225g) grated vegan mozzarella (see the vegan mozzarella recipe on page 26 or use store-bought)

$^2/_3$ cup (55g) grated vegan Parmesan (see the vegan Parmesan recipe on page 112 or use store-bought)

1 tbsp nutritional yeast flakes

salt and freshly ground black pepper

finely chopped chives or flat-leaf parsley, to serve

tempeh "bacon" bits

10 oz (300g) tempeh

2 tbsp pure maple syrup

2 tsp smoked paprika

2 tsp tamari

2 tbsp olive oil

1 To make the tempeh "bacon" bits, crumble the tempeh into tiny pieces. Working in 2 batches, place between two layers of paper towels; squeeze tightly to remove excess moisture. Whisk together the maple syrup, smoked paprika, and tamari in a small bowl. Heat the olive oil in a nonstick skillet over medium heat; cook the tempeh, stirring, for 8 minutes, breaking it up further with a wooden spoon or until lightly browned and very dry. Add the smoked paprika mixture; cook for a further 10 minutes or until dark, dry, and crumbly. Drain on paper towels; season with salt and pepper to taste. Allow to cool.

2 Cook the macaroni in a large saucepan of boiling salted water for 8 minutes or until almost tender; drain. Return the macaroni to the pan.

3 Meanwhile, heat the vegan margarine in a medium saucepan over high heat. Add the flour, smoked paprika, cayenne pepper, and garlic powder; cook, stirring, for 2 minutes or until smooth and combined. Gradually add the macadamia milk, stirring continuously, until the mixture boils and thickens. Stir in the vegan cheeses and nutritional yeast flakes until the cheeses melt; season with salt and pepper to taste.

4 Stir the hot cheese sauce into the hot macaroni until combined. Spoon the macaroni mixture into 4 serving bowls. Serve topped with tempeh "bacon" bits and a sprinkling of chives.

TIPS

- Macadamia milk has a smoother, creamier texture and taste than other dairy-free milks.
- The tempeh "bacon" bits will keep refrigerated for up to 1 week. Scatter over baked sweet potatoes or salads for texture and flavor.

Popcorn cauliflower with spicy tomato sauce

PREP + COOK TIME **1 HOUR** | SERVES **4**

Prepare the spicy tomato sauce the day before to fast-track the recipe for family movie night
or when you are binge-watching your favorite TV programs.

2 tbsp flaxseed meal

1/4 cup (70g) Dijon mustard

2 tbsp hot sauce (see tip)

1²/₃ cups (250g) all-purpose flour

2 tsp onion powder

2 tsp garlic powder

2 tsp smoked paprika

1/2 tsp cayenne pepper

1/2 tsp ground white pepper

1 head of cauliflower (about 3 lbs/1.5kg)

vegetable oil, for deep-frying

salt

lemon wedges, to serve

spicy tomato sauce

2 tbsp vegetable oil

2 tsp brown mustard seeds

1/2 cup (150g) finely chopped onion

2 garlic cloves, sliced

1 tsp ground ginger

1/2 tsp cayenne pepper

1 tsp freshly ground black pepper

1 (15 oz/425g) can crushed tomatoes

1/3 cup (80ml) malt vinegar

1/4 cup (60ml) pure maple syrup

1 To make the spicy tomato sauce, heat the vegetable oil in a saucepan
over medium heat; cook the mustard seeds for 30 seconds or until they
pop. Add the onion, garlic, ginger, cayenne pepper, and black pepper;
cook, stirring, for 5 minutes or until the onion softens. Add the tomatoes,
malt vinegar, maple syrup, and ½ cup (125ml) water; bring to a simmer.
Reduce the heat to low; cook for 25 minutes or until reduced and
thickened. Allow to cool.

2 Combine the flaxseed meal with ²/₃ cup (170ml) water in a large bowl;
allow to stand for 5 minutes or until thickened. Add the Dijon mustard
and hot sauce; stir to combine. In a second large bowl, combine the flour,
onion powder, garlic powder, smoked paprika, cayenne pepper, and white
pepper; season with salt to taste.

3 Cut the cauliflower into 1 to 2-inch (2.5–5cm) florets.

4 Fill a large saucepan one-third full with vegetable oil; heat to 350°F
(180°C) or until a cube of bread dropped into the hot oil turns golden
in 15 seconds. Add the cauliflower to the flaxseed mixture; stir to coat.
Working in batches, toss the cauliflower in the flour mixture to coat.
Carefully lower the coated cauliflower into the hot oil; fry for 2 minutes
or until golden. Drain on paper towels. Season with salt.

5 Serve the cauliflower with the spicy tomato sauce and lemon wedges.

TIP

Use whatever hot sauce you have on hand,
such as sriracha or a Mexican hot sauce.

Spicy black bean and avocado nachos

PREP + COOK TIME **30 MINUTES** | SERVES **2**

Take your taste buds to Mexico with these loaded vegan nachos topped with avocado and fresh pico de gallo. You could also make the nachos with whole grain beet or spinach tortilla chips and kidney beans instead of the black beans, if you'd like.

4 oz (125g) tortilla chips

$^1/_2$ cup (60g) shredded vegan cheddar

$^1/_4$ tsp cumin seeds

2 tsp olive oil

$^1/_3$ cup (100g) finely chopped red onion

1 garlic clove, crushed

2 tsp hot sauce (see tip)

2 tbsp tomato paste

1 (15 oz/425g) can black beans, drained, rinsed

1 tomato (150g), finely chopped

1 long red chile, thinly sliced

1 cup (30g) cilantro leaves

1 tbsp freshly squeezed lime juice

1 avocado (250g)

salt and freshly ground black pepper

lime wedges, to serve

1 Preheat the oven to 350°F (180°C). Line a baking sheet with parchment paper.

2 Place the tortilla chips on the sheet, arranging them in an even layer; scatter over the vegan cheese. Bake for 8 minutes or until the cheese melts and the chips are heated through.

3 Meanwhile, heat a medium sauté pan over medium heat. Add the cumin seeds; stir for 2 minutes or until fragrant. Add the olive oil, onion, and garlic; cook, stirring, for 5 minutes or until the onion is soft. Add the hot sauce and tomato paste; cook, stirring, for 1 minute. Add the black beans and $^1/_3$ cup (80ml) water; cook, stirring, for 2 minutes or until slightly thickened. Lightly mash some of the beans in the pan using a fork or potato masher.

4 Combine the tomato, chile, cilantro, and lime juice in a small bowl. Season with salt and pepper to taste.

5 Spoon the black bean mixture over the tortilla chips. Cut the avocado into slices. Top the nachos with the avocado slices and tomato salsa. Serve with lime wedges.

TIP

Use whatever hot sauce you have on hand, such as green chile or smoky chipotle.

Potato bake with thyme

PREP + COOK TIME **2 HOURS** | SERVES **4**

Use a waxy potato such as Yukon Gold to layer into this delicious, creamy dish. It's a perfect hearty, comforting dish or a side dish for a more substantial meal. The nutritional yeast flakes work double duty, upping the flavor factor and essential B vitamins.

2 tbsp vegan margarine

2 tbsp all-purpose flour

$1/2$ tsp ground nutmeg

4 cups (1 liter) almond milk

2 tbsp nutritional yeast flakes

$2^{1}/_2$ lbs (1.2kg) Yukon Gold or similar potatoes, peeled, thinly sliced

$1/2$ cup (80g) blanched almonds, coarsely chopped

$1/4$ tsp sweet paprika

2 tbsp fresh thyme leaves

salt and freshly ground black pepper

1 Preheat the oven to 350°F (180°C).

2 Heat the margarine in a medium saucepan over medium heat until melted. Add the flour and nutmeg; cook, stirring, for 2 minutes. Reduce the heat to low. Gradually add the almond milk, stirring continuously until smooth. Stir in the nutritional yeast flakes. Increase the heat to medium; cook, stirring, for 10 minutes or until the sauce comes to a simmer. Remove from the heat; season with salt and pepper to taste.

3 Grease a 12-cup (3 liter) ovenproof dish or small Dutch oven. Layer the potatoes in the dish. Pour the white sauce over the potatoes.

4 Cover the dish with foil; bake for 40 minutes. Remove the foil; bake, uncovered, for another 40 minutes. Sprinkle with the almonds and paprika. Return to the oven; bake for a further 10 minutes or until the potatoes are golden.

5 Scatter the potato bake with the thyme; allow to stand for 10 minutes before serving.

TIPS

- You can use sweet potatoes instead of potatoes, but you will need to reduce the cooking time accordingly.
- If you'd like, add bread crumbs at the same time as sprinkling over the almonds for extra crunch on top.

Turmeric dosa with masala cauliflower

PREP + COOK TIME 55 MINUTES + OVERNIGHT STANDING | SERVES 4

Dosa, a South Indian specialty, is made from a fermented batter of rice and legumes. Serve with lime wedges, green chile, and curry leaves briefly fried in a little hot oil, if you'd like.

You will need to start this recipe a day ahead

1 cup (195g) white long-grain rice

$^1/_3$ cup (65g) black lentils (urad dal)

2 tbsp yellow split peas

2 tsp sea salt flakes

$^1/_2$ tsp vegan sugar

1 tsp ground cumin

$^1/_2$ tsp ground turmeric

$^1/_3$ cup (80ml) olive oil, divided

fresh mint chutney

4 cups (80g) mint leaves

2 garlic cloves

2 tbsp grated fresh ginger

3 soft fresh dates (60g), pitted

1 long green chile, coarsely chopped

$^1/_3$ cup (80ml) freshly squeezed lime juice

$^1/_4$ cup (60ml) olive oil

masala cauliflower

1 large head of cauliflower (about 3 lb/1.5kg), cut into small florets

$^1/_3$ cup (80ml) olive oil

$^2/_3$ cup (180g) thinly sliced red onion

1 tsp yellow mustard seeds

1 tsp ground turmeric

$^1/_3$ cup (3g) fresh curry leaves

1 long green chile, thinly sliced

1 tbsp grated fresh ginger

1 To start making the dosas, rinse the rice, lentils, and split peas in a fine mesh strainer under cold running water until the water runs clear; put in a large bowl. Cover generously with water; allow to stand, covered, at room temperature overnight.

2 Strain the rice mixture through a fine mesh strainer. Put the mixture in a food processor with 1$^1/_4$ cups (310ml) water; process until it forms a slightly thick, grainy batter. Transfer to a large bowl. Allow to stand, covered, at room temperature for 4 hours to ferment.

3 To make the mint chutney, add all ingredients to the bowl of a food processor and pulse to a pesto-like consistency. Set aside.

4 To make the masala cauliflower, blanch the cauliflower florets in a large saucepan of boiling water for 3 minutes or until just tender. Drain very well. Heat the olive oil in a large skillet over medium-high heat; cook the onion, stirring, for 5 minutes or until soft. Add the mustard seeds; cook, stirring, for 1 minute or until the seeds start to pop. Add the turmeric, curry leaves, green chile, and ginger; cook, stirring, for 1 minute or until fragrant. Add 2 tablespoons water; stir until combined. Add the drained cauliflower, stir until heated through.

5 Stir the sea salt, sugar, and spices into the fermented dosa batter. If the batter is too thick, add a little extra water.

6 Heat a large nonstick skillet over medium-high heat. Brush the pan lightly with olive oil. Pour $^1/_3$ cup (80ml) batter into the pan. Immediately, and in a circular motion, spread the batter toward the edge of the pan, creating a thin pancake. Drizzle 1 teaspoon of the olive oil around the edges and on the surface of the dosa; cook for 3 minutes or until golden and crisp. Slide a spatula around the edges of the dosa and fold in half; slide onto a plate. Repeat with the remaining batter and olive oil to make 12 dosas total.

7 Fill the dosas with the masala cauliflower; serve with the mint chutney.

Lentil loaf with maple glaze

PREP + COOK TIME **1 HOUR 30 MINUTES** | SERVES **8**

For a shared lunch or light supper, serve this thyme-infused loaf on its own platter with pickled vegetables, beet dip, marinated olives, and cornichons. And you can use the leftovers, should there be any, for a sandwich filling with lettuce and tomato.

1 cup (200g) green lentils, rinsed

$^{1}/_{2}$ cup (100g) brown rice

3 cups (750ml) vegetable stock

1 cup (100g) raw walnuts

1 tbsp olive oil, plus extra for greasing

$^{1}/_{3}$ cup (100g) finely diced red onion

2 celery stalks (200g), finely diced

1 garlic clove, crushed

1 small apple (130g), finely grated

$^{1}/_{4}$ cup (40g) flaxseed meal

$^{3}/_{4}$ cup (90g) rolled oats

$^{1}/_{3}$ cup (8g) thyme leaves, plus extra sprigs to serve

$^{1}/_{3}$ cup (95g) ketchup

2 tbsp pure maple syrup

2 tbsp balsamic vinegar

salt and freshly ground black pepper

1 Preheat the oven to 400°F (200°C). Grease a 9 x 5-inch (23 x 13cm) loaf tin; line with parchment paper.

2 Put the green lentils, brown rice, and vegetable stock in a medium saucepan; bring to a boil. Reduce the heat to medium; simmer gently for 40 minutes or until the lentils and rice are tender and the stock has been absorbed.

3 Meanwhile, put the walnuts on a baking sheet; toast for 4 minutes or until golden. Allow to cool, then coarsely chop. Reduce the oven temperature to 325°F (160°C).

4 Heat the olive oil in a medium skillet; cook the onion and celery, stirring, for 3 minutes or until soft. Add the garlic and apple; cook for 5 minutes. Remove from the heat.

5 Transfer the lentil mixture to a large bowl; add the walnuts and the onion-celery mixture.

6 Combine the flaxseed meal with $^{1}/_{2}$ cup (125ml) water in a small bowl until it becomes a gel-like consistency. Add to the lentil mixture with the rolled oats and the $^{1}/_{3}$ cup (8g) thyme leaves. Season with salt and pepper to taste. Stir well to combine. Spoon the mixture into the prepared loaf pan; smooth the surface.

7 Whisk together the ketchup, maple syrup, and balsamic vinegar in a small bowl. Brush half of the glaze mixture over the top of the loaf. Cover with foil.

8 Bake the loaf for 40 minutes. Remove the foil; brush with the remaining glaze. Bake for a further 20 minutes or until the top is browned. Transfer the pan to a wire rack, and allow the loaf to cool completely before slicing. Serve topped with extra sprigs of thyme.

TIP

A great vegan alternative to meatloaf, the loaf can also be served warm, loaded with mashed potatoes, steamed vegetables, and a vegan gravy.

The botanist burger

PREP + COOK TIME **50 MINUTES + REFRIGERATION** | MAKES **4**

Here it is. Definitive proof that a fabulous vegan burger, sauce, and "crisps"
really can be constructed solely from plant-based food.

2 (15 oz/425g) cans chickpeas, drained, rinsed

2 tbsp chickpea flour (besan)

$^2/_3$ cup (15g) firmly packed flat-leaf parsley leaves

1 cup (25g) firmly packed mint leaves

2 tsp finely grated lemon zest

6 green onions, finely chopped

$^1/_2$ cup (125g) vegan mayonnaise
(see Everyday Mayo on page 55 or use store-bought)

2 garlic cloves, crushed

2 tbsp finely chopped chives

$^1/_2$ lb (240g) zucchini, thinly sliced lengthwise

2 tbsp olive oil, divided

4 seeded sourdough bread rolls, halved

2 small avocados (400g), sliced

2 cups (80g) firmly packed watercress

salt and freshly ground black pepper

kale chips

$^1/_2$ lb (250g) kale

1 tbsp olive oil

sea salt flakes

TIPS

• Save the drained liquid, called aquafaba, from the
canned chickpeas to make vegan meringue (see
page 158) or for the Everyday Mayo on page 55. Store
aquafaba in a container in the fridge for up to 2 days
or freeze for up to 3 months.

• The patties can be made a day ahead; keep in the
fridge, covered, until needed. Or, freeze in an airtight
container, individually wrapped, for up to 2 months.

1 Preheat the oven to 350°F (180°C). Line 2 baking sheets with
parchment paper.

2 Make the kale chips. Remove the stems from the kale; tear the leaves
into medium-sized pieces. Put in a large bowl with oil. Massage the olive
oil into the kale leaves, then arrange them in a single layer on the
prepared sheets. Bake for 10 minutes. Rotate the trays; bake for a further
5 minutes or until the kale is crisp. Allow to cool. Season with salt.

3 Meanwhile, in the bowl of a food processor, process the chickpeas,
chickpea flour, parsley, mint, and lemon zest until the mixture comes
together. Transfer to a medium bowl; stir in the green onions; season
with salt and pepper to taste. Shape the mixture into 4 patties. Place on
a plate; refrigerate for 20 minutes.

4 Clean the bowl of the food processor, then add the vegan mayonnaise
garlic, and chives. Pulse until combined. Set aside.

5 Brush the zucchini with olive oil and place on a hot cast-iron grill pan.
Cook over medium-high heat for 2 minutes on each side or until tender.
Transfer to a plate; cover to keep warm.

6 Brush 1 tablespoon of the olive oil on the same cast-iron grill pan,
then cook the patties for 2 minutes on each side or until browned
and heated through.

7 Brush the insides of each roll with the remaining olive oil and toast on
the cast-iron grill pan.

8 Spoon the mayonnaise mixture onto the bottom half of each roll; top
with the chickpea patties and zucchini. Arrange the avocado over the
zucchini, then top with the watercress. Sandwich each roll with its top
half. Serve with the kale chips.

Daily greens skillet phyllo pie

PREP + COOK TIME 50 MINUTES + COOLING | SERVES 4

Eat a broader diet by rotating the types of greens you eat—such as in this pie—to capture the different valuable nutritional qualities each provides. Serve the pie with dairy-free yogurt or a creamy hummus, or try it with the Beet and Za'atar Dip on page 76, if you'd like.

1¹/₂ lb (750g) Swiss or rainbow chard

¹/₄ cup (60ml) olive oil, divided

1 leek (350g), thinly sliced

3 garlic cloves, crushed

1 tbsp white spelt flour

1 cup (250ml) vegetable stock

2 small zucchini (240g), cut into ¹/₄-in (6mm) slices

¹/₂ lb (250g) Broccolini, cut into 3-in (7.5cm) lengths

1 cup (120g) frozen green peas

6 sheets of phyllo pastry

2 tsp black sesame seeds

2 tsp white sesame seeds

salt and freshly ground black pepper

lemon wedges, to serve

1 Preheat the oven to 425°F (220°C).

2 Trim the ends of the chard stems; chop the stems into ¹/₂-inch (1.25cm) pieces. Coarsely shred the leaves.

3 Heat 2 tablespoons of the olive oil in a 10-inch (25cm) ovenproof skillet over medium heat. Cook the leek and chard stems, stirring occasionally, for 7 minutes or until softened. Add the garlic; cook, stirring, for 1 minute or until fragrant. Add the spelt flour; stir until combined. Gradually stir in the vegetable stock; bring to the boil. Simmer, uncovered, for 2 minutes or until the liquid has slightly thickened.

4 Pour 3 cups boiling water over the shredded chard leaves in a separate large heatproof bowl; allow to stand for 1 minute, then drain. Refresh in another bowl of iced water; drain. Squeeze out as much liquid as possible, then stir into the leek mixture (still in the pan) with the zucchini, Broccolini, and green peas. Season with salt and pepper to taste. Allow to cool for 20 minutes.

5 Brush the phyllo sheets with the remaining olive oil. Loosely scrunch the pastry sheets over the chard mixture in the pan; sprinkle with the black and white sesame seeds. Bake for 15 minutes or until the pastry is golden. Allow the pie to stand for 10 minutes before serving.

TIPS

- This pie can be eaten hot, warm, or cold. To take on a picnic, simply cool, wrap the skillet in a clean kitchen towel, and away you go!
- Make sure the pan you use is nonreactive—that is, not aluminum, pitted, or with any rust spots—to avoid the greens being tainted by a metallic taste.

Veggie patties with beet and caraway chutney

PREP + COOK TIME **1 HOUR + COOLING + REFRIGERATION** | MAKES **6**

These patties are made with millet instead of the usual lentils. The mild-flavored, starchy whole grain is rich in carbs but also contains more calcium than other cereal grains.

$^3/_4$ cup (150g) millet

$^1/_4$ cup (60ml) olive oil

$^1/_4$ cup (80g) finely chopped onion

1 garlic clove, crushed

1-in (2.5cm) piece of fresh ginger (10g), grated

$^1/_2$ lb (225g) sweet potato, peeled, grated

1 cup (160g) frozen corn

2$^1/_2$ cups (75g) baby spinach leaves

$^1/_4$ cup (15g) chopped basil leaves

$^3/_4$ cup (210g) tahini

$^1/_2$ cup (60g) almond meal

grape-seed oil, for frying

6 whole wheat or whole grain slider buns

5 cups (100g) mixed salad greens

$^1/_2$ cup (120g) vegan cashew nut cheese

salt and freshly ground black pepper

beet and caraway chutney

1 tbsp olive oil

$^1/_2$ cup (150g) finely chopped red onion

2 tsp caraway seeds

1 lb (450g) red beets, coarsely grated

$^1/_2$ cup (125ml) apple cider vinegar

$^3/_4$ cup (165g) vegan sugar

$^3/_4$ cup (180ml) coconut water

1 Make the beet and caraway chutney. Heat the olive oil in a medium saucepan over medium heat; cook the onion and caraway seeds, stirring, for 5 minutes or until the onion softens. Add the grated beets, vinegar, sugar, and coconut water; bring to a simmer. Simmer, uncovered, over medium-low heat for 45 minutes or until the grated beet is soft and the mixture is thickened. Season with salt and pepper to taste. Allow to cool.

2 Meanwhile, bring the millet and 3 cups (750ml) water to a boil in a medium saucepan. Reduce the heat to medium; simmer, uncovered, for 15 minutes or until soft. Drain.

3 Heat the olive oil in a large skillet over medium heat; cook the onion, garlic, and ginger, stirring, for 5 minutes or until the onion softens. Add the sweet potato and frozen corn; cook, stirring, for 5 minutes or until the corn is warmed through. Remove from the heat; stir in the spinach. Transfer to a medium bowl; stir in the cooked millet, basil, tahini, and almond meal. Season with salt and pepper to taste.

4 Shape the mixture into 12 patties; place on a baking sheet lined with parchment paper. Refrigerate for 30 minutes.

5 Pour grape-seed oil in a large skillet to $^1/_4$ inch (0.5cm) deep. Heat over medium-high heat. Fry the patties in batches for 3 minutes on each side or until golden. Drain the patties on paper towels.

6 Serve the veggie patties on the bread rolls with the salad greens, cashew nut cheese, and beet and caraway chutney.

TIP

The beet chutney can be made up to a week ahead. Store in an airtight container in the fridge.

Mushroom congee

PREP + COOK TIME **55 MINUTES** | SERVES **6**

In China and Southeast Asia, congee—a warm rice porridge—is the ultimate comfort food.
Rich in B vitamins and zinc and selenium, here shiitake mushrooms add their own comfort.

2 cups (500ml) peanut oil, divided

8 oz (225g) shiitake mushrooms, stalks removed,
4 whole and the rest sliced, divided

5-in (13cm) piece of fresh ginger, thinly sliced

1 cup (215g) sushi rice

8 cups (2 liters) vegetable stock

8 oz (225g) enoki mushrooms, stalks trimmed

6 shallots (150g), thinly sliced

6 large garlic cloves, thinly sliced

2 green onions, thinly sliced

1/2 cup (15g) loosely packed cilantro leaves

1/4 cup (70g) Thai chile jam or chile crisp

2 tsp tamari

2 tsp sesame oil

1 Heat 2 tablespoons of the peanut oil in a large wok over high heat; stir-fry the 4 whole shiitake mushrooms for 4 minutes or until tender; set aside. Stir-fry the sliced shiitake mushrooms and ginger for 4 minutes. Add the rice; stir-fry for a further 2 minutes. Add the vegetable stock and 2 cups (500ml) water; cover the wok, bring to a boil. Uncover; reduce the heat. Simmer, uncovered, for 40 minutes or until the congee is thick like porridge, stirring frequently to avoid it catching on the bottom. With a spoon, skim off and discard any foam from the top during cooking.

2 Meanwhile, heat the remaining oil in a small saucepan to 350°F(180°C) or until a cube of bread dropped into the hot oil turns golden brown in 15 seconds. Fry the enoki mushrooms for 40 seconds or until golden and crisp. Remove from the pan with a slotted spoon; drain on paper towels. Fry the shallots for 2 minutes or until golden and crisp. Remove from the pan with a slotted spoon; drain on paper towels. Fry the garlic for 30 seconds or until just golden. Remove from the pan with a slotted spoon; drain on paper towels. (Be careful not to cook the garlic for too long; otherwise it will become bitter.) In a small bowl, gently toss the cooled enoki, shallot, and garlic with the green onion and cilantro.

3 Serve the congee in bowls, drizzled with the chile jam, tamari, and sesame oil. Top with the whole shiitake mushrooms and fried enoki mixture.

TIPS

- You can buy fried shallots and garlic from Asian grocers to save time.
- Substitute cremini mushrooms for the shiitake mushrooms, if preferred.
- If you have leftover congee, keep refrigerated in an airtight container, separate from the garnishes, for up to 2 days. Reheat with some hot water to loosen the consistency.
- Serve topped with chopped roasted peanuts or cashews for extra protein.

Hoisin baked eggplant with steamed greens

PREP + COOK TIME **40 MINUTES** | SERVES **4**

Use your favorite greens in this recipe—broccoli, bok choy, kale, Swiss chard, asparagus, or even green beans would work well. Be careful not to overcook them because you want them to hold their shape and keep their vibrant color.

2 large eggplants (600g), thickly sliced

1 cup (280g) hoisin sauce

1 tbsp white sesame seeds

2 tsp black sesame seeds

10 oz (275g) buckwheat soba noodles (see tip)

$^1/_2$ cup (125ml) tamari

2 tbsp soft brown sugar

1 tbsp sesame oil

6 oz (175g) Broccolini

5 oz (150g) baby bok choy

thinly sliced green onion, to serve

1 Preheat the oven to 350°F (180°C). Line 2 baking sheets with parchment paper.

2 Arrange the eggplant on the prepared sheets in a single layer; brush both sides with the hoisin sauce. Sprinkle with the white and black sesame seeds. Bake the eggplant for 20 minutes or until tender.

3 Meanwhile, cook the noodles in a large saucepan of boiling salted water for 3 minutes or until just tender. Drain; cover to keep warm.

4 To make the dressing, whisk together the tamari, soft brown sugar, and sesame oil in a small bowl. Put the noodles and half of the dressing in a large bowl; toss to combine.

5 Boil, steam, or microwave the Broccolini and bok choy until tender; drain.

6 Serve the roasted eggplant with the noodles, greens, and remaining dressing. Top with thinly sliced green onion.

TIP

Take care not to overcook the soba noodles; they will continue to cook once drained.

Shepherdless pie

PREP + COOK TIME **1 HOUR** | SERVES **4**

Shepherd's pie is a classic comfort food dish traditionally made with ground lamb topped with mashed potatoes, but who needs lamb when you have lentils, mushrooms, a rainbow of other tasty vegetables, and pillowy polenta? This vegan twist is just as hearty and tasty!

1 cup (200g) French-style green lentils (see tips)

2 tbsp olive oil

$\frac{1}{2}$ cup (150g) coarsely chopped onion

2 garlic cloves, crushed

2 tsp fennel seeds

1 carrot (120g), coarsely chopped

8 oz (225g) cremini or button mushrooms, halved

1 lb (450g) grape tomatoes

2 tbsp tomato paste

1 cup (250ml) vegetable stock

2 cups (60g) baby spinach

salt and freshly ground black pepper

polenta topping

4 cups (1 liter) vegetable stock

1 cup (170g) polenta

2 tbsp finely chopped fresh thyme leaves, plus extra sprigs to serve

2 tbsp olive oil

2 tbsp nutritional yeast flakes

1 Cook the lentils in a medium saucepan of boiling water, uncovered, for 12 minutes or until just tender; drain.

2 Meanwhile, heat the olive oil in a large, deep skillet over medium-high heat. Cook the onion, garlic, and fennel seeds, stirring, for 5 minutes or until the onion is soft. Add the carrot, mushrooms, and tomatoes; cook, covered, for 10 minutes or until the carrot softens. Stir in the tomato paste; cook for 1 minute. Add the vegetable stock; bring to a boil. Cook, uncovered, for 3 minutes or until slightly thickened. Stir in the lentils and spinach; season with salt and pepper to taste. Cover to keep warm.

3 To make the polenta topping, bring the vegetable stock to a boil in a large saucepan. Gradually add the polenta and the chopped thyme to the stock, stirring constantly. Reduce the heat; cook, stirring, for 10 minutes or until the polenta thickens. Stir in the olive oil and nutritional yeast flakes. Season with salt and pepper to taste.

4 Preheat the broiler to high. Put the lentil mixture in an 8-cup (2 liter) ovenproof dish; spread with the polenta topping. Broil for 5 to 10 minutes or until golden and crisp.

5 Serve the pie topped with extra thyme leaves; season with salt and pepper to taste.

TIPS

- French-style green lentils are related to the famed French lentils du Puy; these tiny green-blue lentils have a nutty, earthy flavor and a hardy nature that allows them to be rapidly cooked without disintegrating.
- Use a mixture of Puy and green lentils, if preferred.

SWEET TREATS

Whatever and whenever the occasion, there is something here to soothe your craving, from impressive cakes and candy treats to vegan ice cream and summery tarts.

Citrus poppyseed celebration cake

PREP + COOK TIME **1 HOUR 30 MINUTES + STANDING, COOLING + REFRIGERATION** | SERVES **12**

Hosting a birthday, family party, or holiday celebration? This cake ticks all the boxes for a delicious cake with visual appeal. You can make it in three layers instead of four and change out the fruit for the best of the season.

1 cup (250ml) orange juice

$^1/_3$ cup (50g) poppy seeds

2 cups (500ml) canned coconut milk

1$^1/_2$ tbsp apple cider vinegar

2$^3/_4$ cups (375g) all-purpose flour

2$^1/_2$ tsp baking powder

2 tsp baking soda

$^3/_4$ tsp salt

1$^1/_2$ cups (300g) organic light brown sugar

2 tbsp finely grated orange zest

3 cups (750g) coconut yogurt (use Homemade Coconut Yogurt on page 21 or purchase premade)

8 oz (225g) blueberries, raspberries, blackberries, or other seasonal fruit

3 tsp finely grated lemon zest

1 cup (160g) organic powdered sugar

1$^1/_2$–3 tbsp lemon juice

unsprayed edible flowers (optional)

TIPS

- The cakes can be made a day ahead to the end of step 6; store in an airtight container at room temperature. They can also be frozen for up to 3 months. Allow to thaw when needed, then continue with the recipe.
- To make in three layers, simply prep three 8- or 9-inch (20 or 23cm) cake pans and divide the batter evenly among them. Use a scale for equal portions. Adjust your baking time to 35 to 40 minutes.
- Refrigerate any leftovers.

1 Preheat the oven to 350°F (180°C). Grease and flour 2 deep (9-in/23cm) cake pans. Line the bottom of each pan with parchment paper.

2 Combine the orange juice and poppy seeds in a small bowl; allow to stand for 15 minutes.

3 Meanwhile, combine the coconut milk and apple cider vinegar in a medium bowl; allow to stand for 5 minutes.

4 Sift the flour, baking powder, baking soda, salt, and sugar into a large bowl. Make a well in the center. Add the seed mixture, coconut milk mixture, and orange zest; whisk until just combined. Divide the mixture evenly between the prepared cake pans.

5 Bake the cakes for 45 to 50 minutes or until a toothpick inserted into the center comes out clean. Allow the cakes to cool in the pans for 10 minutes before turning out onto wire racks to cool completely.

6 Split the cakes in half horizontally; refrigerate for 2 hours.

7 For best results, start the final assembly of the cake shortly before you are ready to serve. Place one base layer of cake on a plate. Top with a quarter each of the coconut yogurt, fruit, and lemon zest. Repeat the layering with the remaining cake layers, yogurt, fruit, and lemon zest, finishing with the final cake layer, topped with yogurt.

8 Sift the powdered sugar into a medium bowl; stir in the lemon juice until smooth and the glaze is your desired thickness. Drizzle the glaze over the top of the cake. Top with edible flowers, if you'd like.

Spiced banana bread

PREP + COOK TIME 1 HOUR 15 MINUTES + COOLING | SERVES 10 SLICES

Naturally sweet and fruity, banana bread is easy to make and a tempting treat for
an afternoon snack or even breakfast. This version is less sweet but topped with bananas
that caramelize in the oven as it bakes for a sophisticated take on a classic favorite.

1½ cups (185g) all-purpose flour

1 cup (130g) white spelt flour

1½ tsp baking powder

1 tsp baking soda

1 tsp salt

2 tsp ground cinnamon

1 tsp ground cardamom

1 tsp ground ginger

1 tbsp white chia seeds

³/₄ cup (75g) raw walnuts, coarsely chopped, divided

2 tsp vanilla extract

1 cup (240g) mashed overripe bananas, plus extra
2 just-ripe small bananas (260g), halved lengthwise

³/₄ cup (180ml) almond milk

¹/₃ cup (70g) coconut oil, melted

2 tbsp pure maple syrup, plus extra, to serve (optional)

¹/₂ cup (90g) coconut yogurt (use Homemade Coconut
Yogurt on page 21 or purchase premade)

unsprayed edible flowers (optional)

1 Preheat the oven to 350°F (180°C). Spray a 9 x 4-inch (23 x 10cm) loaf pan
with cooking spray, then line with parchment paper, leaving 2 inches
(5cm) hanging over the sides.

2 Sift the flours, baking powder, baking soda, salt, and spices into a large
bowl; stir in the chia seeds and ¹/₂ cup (50g) of the walnuts. Make a well
in the center. In a separate bowl, combine the vanilla, mashed banana,
almond milk, and coconut oil. Add to the dry ingredients; stir until
just combined.

3 Spread the mixture into the prepared loaf pan. Top with the remaining
¹/₄ cup (25g) walnuts and the extra sliced bananas. Bake for 50 to
60 minutes or until a toothpick inserted into the center comes out
clean. Brush the loaf with the maple syrup. Allow to cool in the pan for
15 minutes before turning out onto a wire rack.

4 Serve slices of the banana bread loaf, warm or cooled, with the coconut
yogurt, drizzled with a little extra maple syrup, and topped with edible
flowers, if you'd like.

TIPS

- For best results, it's important that the bananas
used in the loaf are overripe.
- Loaves tend to crack because of the small surface
area. To test whether a loaf is cooked, insert the
toothpick as close to the center as possible, but
not through a crack; inserting the skewer through
a crack will give an inaccurate result.

Blueberry coconut bars

PREP + COOK TIME **45 MINUTES + FREEZING** | MAKES **12**

Make your own coconut and dark vegan chocolate treats at home. These divine
blueberry-flavored bars are best served at room temperature when the filling will be soft
and moist—it will be difficult to stop at just one!

2¹/₂ cups (200g) dried coconut flakes

5 tbsp (80g) coconut butter, melted

2 tbsp coconut oil, melted

¹/₄ cup (18g) freeze-dried blueberry powder (see tips)

¹/₃ cup (80ml) canned coconut cream

2 tbsp pure maple syrup

chocolate coating

¹/₂ cup (120g) cacao butter

¹/₂ cup (115g) coconut oil

¹/₄ cup (60ml) pure maple syrup

¹/₂ tsp vanilla extract

1 cup (100g) cacao powder

to decorate

1 tbsp dried coconut flakes, finely chopped

¹/₂ tsp freeze-dried blueberry powder

fresh blueberries

edible dried rose petals (optional)

TIPS

- Freeze-dried blueberry powder is available from health food stores and online. Make your own by grinding freeze-dried blueberries in a spice grinder.
- If the chocolate coating thickens, place the bowl over hot water until melted.
- The bars will keep, stored in an airtight container in the freezer, for up to 1 month. Remove from the freezer 45 minutes before eating to soften.

1 Grease a long, narrow loaf pan (at least 10 x 4 in/25 x 10cm), then line with plastic wrap, allowing excess to overhang the sides of the pan.

2 Put the dried coconut flakes in a medium bowl. Using your fingertips, rub in the melted coconut butter and coconut oil until the mixture resembles bread crumbs. Mix in the blueberry powder, then the coconut cream and maple syrup. Evenly press the mixture into the prepared loaf pan; freeze for 30 minutes or until firm.

3 Lifting with the edges of the plastic wrap, remove the coconut mixture from the pan. Cut crosswise into 12 bars. (If you'd like, round the corners of each bar using your hand or a spatula.) Place the bars on a baking sheet lined with parchment paper; freeze while making the coating.

4 To make the chocolate coating, put the cacao butter, coconut oil, maple syrup, and vanilla extract in a medium heatproof bowl over a smaller heatproof bowl of boiling water; whisk until combined. Whisk in the cacao powder until combined and smooth.

5 Working one bar at a time, dip the bars in the chocolate coating, holding the bars underneath with 2 forks. Gently shake off any excess chocolate and return the bars to the baking sheet. Freeze for 10 minutes or until set.

6 Trim off any excess chocolate; double-dip the bars using the leftover chocolate. Return to the freezer to set for 10 minutes, and trim again.

7 To decorate, combine the coconut and blueberry powder in a small bowl, and sprinkle over the bars in a line. Decorate with fresh blueberries and dried rose petals, if you'd like.

Strawberries-and-cream "cheesecake"

PREP TIME 1 HOUR 10 MINUTES + STANDING + REFRIGERATION | SERVES 16

Pretty as a picture, this dreamy, creamy no-bake "cheesecake" is simply delectable. Just remember that you need to start this recipe at least a day ahead to allow time for it to set.

You will need to start this recipe at least a day ahead

2½ cups (375g) raw cashews

1 cup (140g) raw macadamias

¾ cup (60g) dried coconut flakes

½ cup (60g) almond meal

6 soft fresh dates (120g), pitted

1 tsp salt

¾ tsp vanilla extract, divided

¾ cup (150g) coconut oil, melted, divided

1 lb (450g) small strawberries, plus extra halved to serve

1 cup (240g) coconut yogurt (use Homemade Coconut Yogurt on page 21 or purchase premade)

½ cup (125ml) light agave syrup

1 tbsp finely grated lemon zest

⅓ cup (80ml) lemon juice

⅓ cup (80g) cacao butter, melted

coconut flakes and unsprayed edible flowers, to serve (optional)

TIPS

- If you have one, use a high-powered blender in steps 5 and 6 to achieve a really smooth result.
- The cheesecake will keep in an airtight container in the fridge for up to 4 days.

1 Put the cashews in a medium bowl with enough cold water to cover. Allow to stand, covered, for 4 hours. Drain, then rinse under cold water. Drain well a second time.

2 Grease a 9-inch (23cm) round springform pan. Line the bottom with a round of parchment paper, then line the side of the pan with a 3-inch (7.5cm) strip of parchment paper.

3 In the bowl of a food processor, combine the macadamias, dried coconut flakes, almond meal, dates, salt, and ¼ teaspoon vanilla. Pulse until the mixture resembles coarse crumbs. Add 1 tablespoon of the coconut oil; process until combined and the mixture starts to stick together. Press the mixture into the bottom of the lined pan. Next, using the back of a spoon, press down firmly and level to form the cheesecake base.

4 Hull then thinly slice the strawberries lengthwise. The strawberries shouldn't be taller than the side of the pan. Trim any to make them all the same height. Place the tallest strawberry slices around the side of the cake pan, sticking them to the parchment paper; reserve the remaining slices. Refrigerate the tin until needed.

5 In a blender, blend the drained cashews with the coconut yogurt, agave syrup, lemon zest, lemon juice, and the remaining ½ teaspoon vanilla extract until as smooth as possible. Add the cacao butter and the remaining coconut oil; blend again until as smooth as possible. Pour two-thirds of the cashew mixture over the cheesecake base; smooth the surface. Refrigerate while preparing the strawberry layer.

6 Blend the reserved strawberry slices until as smooth as possible; stir into the remaining cashew mixture. Gently spoon the strawberry-cashew mixture over the cream layer; do not pour, or the layers will combine. Refrigerate overnight or until set.

7 Remove the cheesecake from the pan and place on a plate to serve. Top with halved extra strawberries and sprinkle with coconut flakes and edible flowers, if you'd like.

Strawberry mylkshake popsicles

PREP TIME 25 MINUTES + STANDING + FREEZING | MAKES 8

Perfect for a sweltering summer's day, these luscious popsicles are made with vegan mylk
or "malk." They're best made with strawberries at their ripest, with a strong aroma and taste,
so that they infuse the popsicles with the maximum amount of flavor.

You will need to start this recipe a day ahead

$1/4$ cup (40g) raw cashews

$1^2/3$ cups (400ml) canned coconut cream

$1/4$ cup (60ml) pure maple syrup

1 tsp pure vanilla extract

8 oz (225g) strawberries, hulled

chocolate coating

$1/4$ cup (50g) coconut oil

$1/4$ cup (60g) cacao butter, chopped

2 tbsp pure maple syrup

$1/2$ cup (50g) cacao powder

TIPS

- If you have one, use a high-powered blender in step 2; this type of blender will produce a very smooth consistency.

- To create thin drizzled lines of chocolate on the popsicles, use a plastic resealable bag. Spoon the melted chocolate coating into the bag, then cut off a tiny tip at one corner of the bag. Drizzle the chocolate over the popsicles. Freeze for 5 minutes or until set; turn over and repeat.

- Store the popsicles in an airtight container, placing a sheet of parchment paper between them. The popsicles can be frozen for up to 2 months.

1   Put the cashews in a medium bowl; cover with cold water. Allow to stand, covered, for 4 hours or overnight. Drain the cashews, then rinse under cold water; drain well.

2   In a blender, blend the drained cashews with the coconut cream, maple syrup, vanilla extract, and strawberries until as smooth as possible.

3   Pour the mixture into 8 ($1/3$-cup/80ml) popsicle molds; freeze for 1 hour. Insert popsicle sticks; freeze overnight or until firm.

4   Run the molds briefly under cold water; remove the popsicles. Place the popsicles on a baking sheet lined with parchment paper; return to the freezer with the popsicles still on the baking sheet.

5   Make the chocolate coating. Put the coconut oil and cacao butter in a medium heatproof bowl over a smaller heatproof bowl of boiling water. Whisk until combined and smooth, then whisk in the maple syrup. Whisk in the cacao powder until combined and smooth. Pour the chocolate into a small, wide glass; this will make it easier to dip the popsicles.

6   Dip the tips of the popsicles, one at a time, into the chocolate coating. Gently shake off any excess chocolate. Return to the parchment-lined baking sheet; freeze for 5 minutes or until the chocolate is firm. If you want to alternate the chocolate pattern, drizzle some of the popsicles with chocolate (see tips).

Popcorn rocky road bark

PREP + COOK TIME **15 MINUTES + FREEZING** | SERVES **8**

Simple to put together and even easier to eat, this no-bake slice fuses two much-loved snack foods into one decadent confection. Coconut oil has a low melting point and the rice malt syrup keeps the bark soft, so you need to eat these treats while they are still frozen.

½ cup (100g) coconut oil

½ cup (50g) cacao powder

½ cup (175g) rice malt syrup

1 tbsp almond butter

2 tsp vanilla extract

1½ cups (25g) salted popcorn, divided

1 cup (50g) coconut flakes, divided

¾ cup (125g) dry-roasted almonds, divided

⅓ cup (45g) dried sweetened cranberries, divided (see tip)

1 Line 9 x 4-inch (23 x 10cm) loaf pan with parchment paper, allowing the edges to overhang 2 inches (5cm) over the sides of the pan.

2 Melt the coconut oil in a medium saucepan over low heat. Remove from the heat; whisk in the cacao powder, rice malt syrup, almond butter, and vanilla until all ingredients are dissolved and the mixture is smooth.

3 Stir in three-quarters each of the popcorn, flaked coconut, almonds, and cranberries. Spoon the mixture into the prepared pan; spread evenly over the bottom. Scatter with the remaining popcorn, flaked coconut, almonds ,and cranberries; press lightly into the cocoa mixture to secure.

4 Freeze the bark for 15 minutes or until frozen solid.

5 Cut the frozen bark into slices or chunks. Eat immediately, frozen, or store in an airtight container in the freezer for up to 1 month.

TIP

You can use freeze-dried strawberries or raspberries instead of the cranberries.

Frozen no-bake blueberry meringue slab pie

PREP + COOK TIME **40 MINUTES + FREEZING** | SERVES **8**

Aquafaba, in this case the water drained from a can of chickpeas, is used to make the vegan-friendly meringue topping this dessert. To brown the meringue, you will need a kitchen blowtorch, available from kitchen supply stores or online.

1 cup (90g) rolled oats

1 cup (160g) raw almonds, roasted

$^3/_4$ cup (175g) soft medjool dates

$^1/_4$ cup (60ml) olive oil

1 tbsp pure maple syrup

$^1/_2$ tsp sea salt flakes

2 cups (300g) frozen blueberries

10 oz (300g) silken tofu

1 cup (275ml) canned coconut cream

$^1/_2$ cup (120g) agave nectar

1 tsp vanilla extract

2 limes (130g), zest cut into strips, juiced, divided

fresh blueberries, to serve (optional)

Italian meringue

1 cup (220g) vegan cane sugar

1 (15 oz/425g) can chickpeas, unopened

2 tsp cream of tartar

TIPS

- Use the chickpeas for recipes such as Avocado Toast with Smoky Chickpeas (page 40) or Wasabi Edamame Hummus Pack (page 86).
- If you don't have a kitchen blowtorch, place the dessert under the broiler for 30 seconds or until the meringue is lightly browned.

1 Line a 9 x 4-inch (23 x 10cm) loaf pan with two layers of parchment paper, allowing the parchment to overhang the long sides by 2 inches (5cm).

2 In the bowl of a food processor, process the rolled oats, almonds, dates, oil, maple syrup, and salt until coarsely combined and sticking together well. Press the mixture evenly and firmly into the bottom of the pan.

3 Clean the bowl of the food processor, then add the blueberries, tofu, coconut cream, agave nectar, vanilla extract, and $^1/_4$ cup (60ml) of the lime juice; process until smooth. Pour into the loaf pan; freeze for 2 hours or until set.

4 To make the Italian meringue, put the sugar and $^1/_3$ cup (80ml) water in a small saucepan; stir gently. Place the pan over medium heat; cook without stirring for 15 minutes or until the syrup reaches 244°F (118°C) on a cooking thermometer.

5 Meanwhile, strain the chickpeas through a sieve set over a small bowl; you should have $^3/_4$ cup (180ml) chickpea liquid (aquafaba). Reserve the chickpeas for another use (see tips). Put the aquafaba in the bowl of an stand mixer. Whisk on high speed until tripled in volume, then whisk in the cream of tartar.

6 When the sugar syrup has reached temperature, slowly pour into the meringue mixture. Increase the speed to a maximum; whisk for a further 3 minutes or until the bowl feels room temperature to touch.

7 Spoon the Italian meringue over the blueberry layer; using the back of a spoon, swirl the meringue to form peaks. Using a blowtorch, lightly brown the meringue (see tips). Return to the freezer for 30 minutes or until ready to serve.

8 Serve topped with the lime zest and extra fresh blueberries, if you'd like.

Giant brownie sundae

PREP + COOK TIME **45 MINUTES** | SERVES **4**

What chocolate lover could resist this brownie-meets-sundae extravaganza where everyone can dig in to their heart's content? You can go the whole nine yards and add all the extras— chocolate sauce, ice cream, and toppings—or keep it simple.

1 cup plus 3 tbsp (150g) all-purpose flour, divided

1/2 cup (110g) firmly packed coconut palm sugar

1/2 cup (110g) vegan cane sugar

3/4 cup (65g) cocoa powder

1/3 cup (80ml) vegetable oil

1 tsp vanilla extract

1/2 tsp sea salt flakes

1 tsp baking powder

21/2 oz (75g) vegan chocolate, chopped

4 scoops of chocolate dairy-free ice cream

8 vegan sugar wafer cookies

1/2 cup (50g) vegan mini chocolate sandwich cookies

8 maraschino cherries with stems (see tip)

chocolate sauce

1/4 cup (60ml) pure maple syrup

1/2 cup (50g) cocoa powder

1 tbsp coconut oil

1 tsp vanilla extract

1 Preheat the oven to 350°F (180°C). Grease a 9-inch (23cm) cast-iron skillet or round cake pan.

2 Put 1/4 cup (40g) of the flour and 1/2 cup (125ml) water in a saucepan over medium heat; cook, whisking continuously, until the mixture thickens. Transfer to a bowl; allow to cool.

3 In a large bowl, stir together the sugars, cocoa powder, vegetable oil, vanilla, and sea salt. Add the cooked flour mixture; stir until well combined. Stir in the combined remaining sifted flour and baking powder, followed by the chopped chocolate. (The mixture will be very thick. You may need to use your hands.)

4 Press the brownie mixture into the prepared skillet or pan; bake for 20 minutes or until a toothpick inserted in the center comes out clean.

5 Meanwhile, make the chocolate sauce. Put the ingredients in a small saucepan. Add 1/2 cup (125ml) water. Bring to a simmer, whisking occasionally until smooth, for 5 minutes. Allow to cool. (The sauce will thicken on cooling.)

6 Top the brownie with the scoops of chocolate dairy-free ice cream, wafer cookies, sandwich cookies, and maraschino cherries; drizzle with the chocolate sauce.

TIP

Check the label to ensure the maraschino cherries you choose are suitable for vegans, or use Amarena cherries in syrup instead.

Fruity soft serves

PREP TIME **20 MINUTES + FREEZING** | MAKES **12**

Impress family and friends with these refreshing frozen treats on a hot day. They are easy to make and have very little, if any, added sugar. Just make sure you start early in the day because the fruit purees have to freeze for at least 4 hours before piping to serve.

You will need to start this recipe at least 4 hours ahead

avocado and lime

3 large avocados (960g), halved, pitted, chopped

$^{1}/_{3}$ cup (80ml) freshly squeezed lime juice

$^{2}/_{3}$ cup (105g) vegan powdered sugar

1 tsp finely grated lime zest

banana and raspberry

8 oz (225g) frozen raspberries

2 lbs (800g) overripe bananas, coarsely chopped

mango and passion fruit

2 lb (800g) frozen diced mango

$^{1}/_{4}$ cup (60g) passion fruit pulp

1 To make the avocado and lime soft serve, in the bowl of a food processor, process the avocado, lime juice, and powdered sugar until very smooth. Pour the puree into a large resealable bag; seal. Freeze flat for 4 hours or until the puree is solid. Break the frozen puree into chunks, and process again until smooth. Spoon the soft serve into a piping bag fitted with a large star tip. Immediately pipe the mixture into cups or ice cream cones; sprinkle with the lime zest to serve. (Makes 2$^{1}/_{2}$ cups)

2 To make the banana and raspberry soft serve, put the frozen raspberries in the bowl of a food processor; pulse briefly to roughly crumble. Remove a quarter of the raspberries; reserve in the freezer until ready to serve. Add the banana to the remaining raspberries; process until very smooth. Pour into a large resealable bag; seal. Freeze flat for 4 hours or until the puree is solid. Break the frozen puree into chunks, and process again until smooth. Spoon the soft serve into a piping bag fitted with a large star tip. Immediately pipe the mixture into cups or ice cream cones; sprinkle with the frozen crumbled raspberries to serve. (Makes 2$^{1}/_{2}$ cups)

3 To make the mango and passion fruit soft serve, in the bowl of a food processor, process the mango until very smooth. Add half of the passion fruit pulp; pulse until well combined. Pour into a large resealable bag; seal. Freeze flat for 4 hours or until the puree is solid. Break the frozen puree into chunks, and process again until smooth. Spoon the soft serve into a piping bag fitted with a large star tip. Immediately pipe the mixture into small cups or ice cream cones. Drizzle with the remaining passion fruit pulp to serve. (Makes 3$^{1}/_{2}$ cups)

TIPS

- To pipe the soft serves, you need 3 (16-in/40cm) disposable piping bags and 1 large star tip.
- The soft serve can be stored in the piping bags in the freezer for up to 2 hours before becoming too firm to pipe.

Overnight jasmine tea and lemon curd rolls

PREP + COOK TIME **45 MINUTES + OVERNIGHT REFRIGERATION** | MAKES **12**

The tea-infused dough for these pull-apart rolls is left to rise slowly in the fridge overnight before being shaped and baked the next day.

You will need to start this recipe a day ahead

3 green tea with jasmine teabags

1 tsp finely grated lemon zest, plus extra to serve

2 tbsp pure maple syrup, divided

3 cups (480g) bread flour

1 packet (2$\frac{1}{4}$ tsp) instant yeast

1$\frac{1}{2}$ tsp sea salt flakes

1 tsp ground cardamom

chopped pistachios, to serve (optional)

nut filling

$\frac{1}{2}$ cup (70g) pistachios, coarsely chopped

$\frac{1}{2}$ cup (40g) shredded coconut, toasted

$\frac{1}{2}$ cup (110g) firmly packed vegan brown sugar

lemon curd

$\frac{1}{3}$ cup (80ml) lemon juice

1 tbsp cornstarch

1 cup (250ml) canned coconut cream

$\frac{1}{4}$ cup (60ml) pure maple syrup

$\frac{1}{8}$ tsp ground turmeric

1 Put the jasmine green tea teabags in a heatproof bowl with 1$\frac{2}{3}$ cups (410ml) boiling water. Steep for 30 minutes or until the water is lukewarm. Remove the teabags; discard. Stir the lemon zest and 1 tablespoon of the maple syrup into the tea.

2 Combine the flour, yeast, sea salt, and cardamom in a large bowl. Make a well in the center. Pour the tea mixture into the well; mix to a sticky dough. Transfer the dough to a large oiled bowl; cover with plastic wrap. Refrigerate for 12 hours or overnight.

3 Make the nut filling. Combine the ingredients in a small bowl.

4 Turn out the dough onto a well-floured work surface; press out to a 9 x 16-inch (23 x 40cm) rectangle. Scatter the nut filling over. Starting from one long end, tightly roll up the dough to enclose the filling, tucking in the ends. Cut the log into 12 pieces. Place each piece, cut-side up, in a greased 9-inch (23cm) cake pan. Cover loosely. Allow to stand in a warm place for 1 hour or until the dough has increased in size by one-third.

5 Meanwhile, make the lemon curd. Whisk the lemon juice and cornstarch in a small saucepan over medium heat until smooth. Whisk in the coconut cream, maple syrup, and turmeric until combined; cook, whisking continuously, until the mixture boils and thickens slightly. Reduce the heat slightly; continue whisking for a further 5 minutes or until the mixture is thick enough to coat the back of a spoon. Transfer to a bowl; cover the surface directly with plastic wrap. Chill until needed.

6 Preheat the oven to 400°F (200°C). Bake the scrolls for 25 to 30 minutes. Brush the tops with the remaining 1 tablespoon maple syrup; bake for a further 5 minutes or until shiny and glossy.

7 Drizzle the rolls with 2 tablespoons of the lemon curd; top with extra grated lemon zest and chopped pistachios, if you'd like. Serve with the remaining lemon curd.

Coconut and strawberry "panna cotta"

PREP + COOK TIME **25 MINUTES + REFRIGERATION** | SERVES **4**

A very vegan version of panna cotta, this fresh-flavored dessert has only four ingredients and can be made ahead of time if you are entertaining. Serve it in glasses or jars so that the lovely pastel shades of the coconut and strawberry layers are shown off.

4 young coconuts (4kg in total) (see tip)

1/2 tsp agar agar powder (see tips)

8 oz (225g) strawberries

1 tbsp freshly squeezed lemon juice

unsprayed edible flowers (optional)

1 Place one of the coconuts on its side on a cutting board; carefully cut off the dome-shaped top with a large knife—you will need to use a bit of force. Drain the coconut water into a large bowl. Spoon out the soft flesh. Repeat with the remaining coconuts; you should end up with about 2 cups (280g) of flesh.

2 In a high-powered blender, blend the coconut flesh with 1 cup (250ml) of the coconut water until as smooth as possible to form a puree.

3 Combine 1 cup (250ml) of the coconut water and the agar agar powder in a small saucepan. (Reserve any leftover coconut water for another use.) Bring to a simmer, stirring, over low heat; simmer for 5 minutes. Add to the coconut puree; blend until well combined.

4 Pour two-thirds of the coconut puree into 4 (1-cup/250ml) glasses or jars, dividing the mixture evenly. Refrigerate for 10 minutes or until slightly set.

5 Reserve half of the strawberries for serving; refrigerate. Hull the remaining strawberries; add to the remaining coconut puree with the juice. Blend until as smooth as possible. Carefully pour over the set coconut mixture; refrigerate for 4 hours or until both layers are set.

6 Serve topped with the reserved sliced or halved strawberries and edible flowers.

TIPS

- If you don't have access to coconuts, you can use 2 cups (280g) of fresh coconut and 2 cups (500ml) of coconut water.
- Agar agar powder is available from large grocery stores, health food shops, and online. Derived from seaweed, it is a vegan/vegetarian substitute for gelatin.
- You can store the panna cotta in the fridge for up to 4 days.

Ginger, coconut, and almond bars

PREP + COOK TIME 45 MINUTES + STANDING + REFRIGERATION | MAKES **16**

Ginger lovers rejoice! This vegan-friendly bar is layered with creamy coconut and topped with toasted flaked almonds and crystallized ginger. Use the leftover coconut water as a base for fruity summer drinks, for cooking rice, or in Berry Basket Cream Tarts (page 172).

You will need to start this recipe a day ahead

1½ cups (225g) raw cashews

1½ cups (240g) raw almonds

1 cup (140g) pitted dried dates, coarsely chopped

½ cup (40g) shredded coconut

½ cup (90g) fresh flake coconut

¾ cup (165g) crystallized ginger, thinly sliced, divided

¾ cup (180ml) melted coconut oil, divided

½ cup (125ml) rice malt syrup, divided

2 tbsp finely grated fresh ginger

½ cup (125ml) canned coconut cream

1½ tsp vanilla extract

2 tbsp sliced almonds, toasted, to serve

1 Put the cashews in a medium bowl; cover with cold water. Allow to stand, covered, for 1 hour. Drain the cashews, rinse under cold water; drain well.

2 Line the bottom and sides of 9 x 9-inch (23 x 23cm) baking dish or cake pan with parchment paper, extending the edges 2 inches (5cm) over the sides.

3 In the bowl of a food processor, process the drained cashews and almonds until finely chopped. Add the dates, shredded coconut, ¼ cup (55g) of the crystallized ginger, ¼ cup (60ml) of the coconut oil, and 1 tablespoon of the rice malt syrup; pulse until combined. Press the mixture over the bottom of the prepared pan. Refrigerate until needed.

4 In a blender, blend or process the fresh coconut, fresh ginger, coconut cream, vanilla extract, the remaining coconut oil, the remaining rice malt syrup, and ¼ cup (55g) of the crystallized ginger until smooth. Pour the mixture over the biscuit crust. Refrigerate overnight.

5 Cut into bars; serve topped with the sliced almonds and remaining ¼ cup (55g) crystallized ginger.

TIP

The bar keeps well in an airtight container in the fridge for up to 1 week or can be frozen for up to 2 months; thaw in the fridge.

Peppermint bites

PREP TIME **45 MINUTES + STANDING, FREEZING + REFRIGERATION** | MAKES **15**

Activated buckwheat groats (also called buckinis) add a crunchy layer to these no-bake beauties. Sweet, creamy peppermint filling and bitter chocolate perfectly satisfy a craving.

You will need to start this recipe a day ahead

³/₄ cup (115g) raw cashews

¹/₂ cup (80g) raw almonds

¹/₂ cup (60g) raw pecans

¹/₃ cup (65g) activated buckwheat groats

²/₃ cup (50g) dried shredded coconut

¹/₂ cup (50g) cacao powder

¹/₄ cup (40g) vegan coconut palm sugar

2 tsp mesquite flour (see tips)

4 soft fresh dates (80g), pitted

²/₃ cup (140g) coconut oil, melted, divided

¹/₄ cup (60ml) canned coconut cream

2 tbsp agave syrup

¹/₂ tsp pure peppermint extract

chocolate coating

¹/₄ cup (50g) coconut oil

¹/₄ cup (60g) cacao butter, chopped

2 tbsp pure maple syrup

¹/₂ cup (50g) cacao powder

TIPS

- Mesquite flour, also called mesquite powder, is a sweetener with a molasses, nutty, spicy flavor. Look for it at organic grocery stores or online.
- Store in an airtight container in the fridge for up to 5 days.x

1 Put the cashews in a medium bowl; cover with cold water. Allow to stand, covered, for 4 hours or overnight. Drain the cashews, rinse under cold water; drain well and set aside.

2 Lightly grease a 9 x 9-inch (23 x 23cm) baking dish, then line with plastic wrap extending it 1 inch (2.5cm) above the sides.

3 In a food processor, process the almonds, pecans, buckwheat groats, shredded coconut, cacao powder, sugar, mesquite flour, dates, and ¹/₂ cup (125ml) of the coconut oil until coarse crumbs form and the mixture starts to clump. Press the mixture firmly and evenly over the bottom of the pan using a spatula to form a ¹/₄-inch- (6mm) thick layer. Freeze for 15 minutes or until firm.

4 Lift the base from the dish and place on a cutting board. Cut into 15 rounds using a 2-inch (5cm) round cookie cutter. Place the rounds on a baking sheet lined with parchment paper; freeze while preparing the peppermint cream.

5 To make the peppermint cream, blend the drained cashews with the remaining coconut oil, coconut cream, and agave syrup until as smooth as possible. Add the peppermint extract; blend until combined. Pour the peppermint cream into a small bowl. Cover, then freeze, stirring occasionally, for 1 hour or until thick but not set.

6 Spoon 2 teaspoons of peppermint cream onto each biscuit round; using the back of the teaspoon, gently press down to flatten and smooth. Freeze for 3 hours or until set.

7 Make the chocolate coating. Put the coconut oil and cacao butter in a medium heatproof bowl over a smaller heatproof bowl of boiling water, whisk until combined and smooth; whisk in the maple syrup. Whisk in the cacao powder until combined and smooth. Pour into a small bowl.

8 Using a fork, lower the cookies one at a time into the chocolate mixture. Allow any excess chocolate to drip off, then place each on the baking sheet. Refrigerate for 30 minutes or until the chocolate is set.

Berry basket cream tarts

PREP + COOK TIME **50 MINUTES + STANDING, COOLING + REFRIGERATION** | MAKES **6**

These luscious nut-cream-filled tarts are the answer to all vegan dreams of being able to eat a beautiful creamy French-style fruit tart. To make the most of their taste and aroma, choose the best, most perfectly ripe fruit you can find to top the tarts.

You will need to start this recipe at least 4 hours ahead

2 cups (320g) raw almonds

3/4 cup (100g) pitted medjool dates

1 tbsp coconut oil, melted

1 tbsp psyllium husks

1–2 tbsp coconut water

3/4 tsp salt

1/2 cup (100g) raspberries

1/2 cup (65g) small strawberries, halved

1/2 cup (75g) blueberries

1/2 cup (100g) cherries, halved

1/4 cup unsprayed edible flowers (optional)

pastry cream

2 1/2 cups (350g) raw macadamias

2/3 cup (160ml) agave syrup

3/4 cup (180ml) coconut water

2 tsp finely grated orange zest

2 tsp vanilla extract

3/4 cup (150g) coconut oil, melted

1 Preheat the oven to 325°F (160°C). Grease 6 (4 1/2-in/12cm) mini pie pans or ramekins.

2 Make the pastry cream. Put the macadamias in a medium bowl; cover with cold water. Allow to stand for 4 hours or overnight; drain. Rinse the macadamias; drain well. Put the soaked macadamias in a high-powered blender with the remaining ingredients for the pastry cream; blend until smooth.

3 Process the almonds, dates, coconut oil, psyllium husks, and enough of the coconut water to ensure the mixture forms a coarse paste and clumps together.

4 Press 1/3 cup of the nut mixture firmly over the bottom and side of each pie dish. Place the dishes on a large baking sheet. Bake for 15 minutes or until lightly browned; allow to cool.

5 Divide the pastry cream evenly among the crusts. Cover, then refrigerate for 4 hours or overnight until set.

6 Serve the tarts topped with the fresh fruit and sprinkled with edible flowers, if you'd like.

TIP

The tarts can be made a day ahead; keep covered in the fridge. Decorate with the berries and flowers, if using, just before serving.

Rice pudding with poached rhubarb and plums

PREP + COOK TIME **50 MINUTES + COOLING** | SERVES **6**

Wonderfully versatile, rice pudding makes for a perfect dessert. You can even serve this vegan-friendly version for brunch. Rich and creamy thanks to oat milk and coconut nectar, it's topped with sweet poached rhubarb and plums for a vibrant touch.

2 tbsp pistachios

3 oranges (720g)

2 tbsp vegan margarine spread

$^3/_4$ cup (160g) sushi rice

4 cups (1 liter) oat milk or other dairy-free milk (see tips)

$^1/_3$ cup (80ml) coconut nectar

2 tsp vanilla extract

poached rhubarb and plums

4 cups (1 liter) apple juice

2 tbsp coconut nectar

1 cinnamon stick

4 star anise

3 large rhubarb stems (300g), trimmed, cut into 3-in (7.5cm) lengths

4 small blood plums (300g), quartered, seeded

TIPS

• You can use any dairy-free milk except for almond milk for the rice pudding. Oat milk is a good choice, as is coconut milk—although you may need a little more, as this is thicker than other dairy-free milks.

• If the stems of the rhubarb are thin, reduce the cooking time accordingly.

• The rice pudding and poached fruit can be made a day ahead; keep refrigerated, separately, until needed. Reheat the rice pudding with a little more of your chosen dairy-free milk for a creamy mixture.

1 Make the poached rhubarb and plums. Bring the apple juice, coconut nectar, cinnamon, and star anise to a simmer in a medium saucepan over medium heat. Add the rhubarb and plums; simmer, uncovered, for 2 minutes. Be careful not to boil the fruit or it will become mushy. Remove the fruit from the pan with a slotted spoon; transfer to a heatproof bowl. Peel the plums; discard the skins. Bring the syrup to a boil, then reduce the heat and simmer, uncovered, for 30 minutes or until reduced to 1 cup (250ml). Allow to cool slightly. Serve warm.

2 Meanwhile, preheat the oven to 350°F (180°C). Spread the pistachios over a baking sheet; roast for 5 minutes or until lightly browned, or put the pistachios in a skillet and toast over medium-low heat, stirring, until lightly browned.

3 Remove the zest from one of the oranges using a zester. Alternatively, peel the zest thinly from the orange, avoiding the white pith. Cut the zest into long, thin strips. Set aside until needed. Squeeze the juice from the oranges; you will need 1 cup (250ml).

4 Melt the margarine in a large deep skillet over medium heat. Add the sushi rice; cook, stirring, for 2 minutes. Add the orange juice, oat milk, coconut nectar, and vanilla extract; bring to a boil. Reduce the heat to a simmer. Cook, uncovered, stirring occasionally for 20 minutes or until the rice is tender and the mixture is thick.

5 Spoon the rice mixture into 6 ($1^1/_2$-cup/375ml) bowls. Serve topped with the poached fruit and warm fruit syrup, sprinkled with toasted pistachios and reserved orange zest.

Fudgy sweet potato brownies with espresso sauce

PREP + COOK TIME **1 HOUR 30 MINUTES** | MAKES **16**

These rich brownies yield an especially gooey result made even more decadent
by the espresso sauce. Ground flaxseed helps to make it more healthy.

1 lb (450g) sweet potato, peeled, chopped
(about 1½ cups)

2 tbsp ground flaxseed meal

½ cup (125ml) hot water

6 oz (180g) vegan dark chocolate (70% cocoa),
chopped

1¼ cups (200g) vegan coconut palm sugar

2 tsp vanilla extract

2 tbsp cacao powder

1 cup (120g) almond meal

¼ tsp baking soda

espresso sauce

2 tsp instant coffee granules

1 tbsp boiling water

⅓ cup (80ml) pure maple syrup

⅓ cup (55g) vegan coconut palm sugar

1 tbsp (20g) vegan dark chocolate (70% cocoa),
chopped

¼ cup (50g) coconut oil

2 tsp vanilla extract

¼ cup (25g) cacao powder

TIPS

- The sauce thickens quickly on standing. Reheat
gently to return to a thin consistency.
- These brownies are delicious at room temperature
and last for up to 3 days in an airtight container in
the fridge. Bring to room temperature before serving.
They can also be frozen for up to 2 months.

1 Put the sweet potato in a medium saucepan with enough cold water to
cover; bring to the boil. Cook, covered, for 15 minutes or until soft. Drain;
return to the saucepan. Mash until smooth.

2 Meanwhile, preheat the oven to 350°F (180°C). Grease and flour a 9 x
9-inch (23 x 23cm) baking dish or cake pan.

3 Combine the flaxseed meal and the hot water in a small heatproof bowl.
Allow to stand for 10 minutes.

4 Put the chocolate, sugar, vanilla extract, ¼ cup (60ml) water, and sifted
cacao powder in a large heatproof bowl over a saucepan of simmering
water. Stir until melted and smooth. Remove from the heat; stir in the
mashed sweet potato. Add the flaxseed meal mixture, almond meal, and
baking soda; mix well. Pour the mixture into the prepared pan. Bake for
60 to 70 minutes or until firm to the touch. Allow to cool slightly for
10 minutes in the pan.

5 Make the espresso sauce. Dissolve the coffee in the boiling water.
Combine the maple syrup, coconut sugar, chocolate, coconut oil, vanilla
extract, and coffee in a small saucepan over low heat; stir until melted
and smooth. Remove from the heat; stir in the sifted cacao powder.

6 Pour the espresso sauce over the brownie layer. Let cool for 30 minutes.
Cut the warm brownies into squares. Serve topped with sweet potato
peace signs, if you'd like (see below).

peace-sign brownies To decorate the brownie squares with individual
sweet potato peace signs, peel and slice 1 sweet potato (300g) into ⅛ inch
(3mm) thick slices. Using a 1-inch (2.5cm) pastry cutter, cut into rounds.
Heat 2 teaspoons coconut oil in a large skillet over high heat, then cook
the sweet potato for 2 minutes on each side until just tender. Pour in 1
tablespoon coconut syrup, and cook for another minute until slightly
caramelized. Cut each sweet potato round into peace symbols, as
pictured opposite.

Caramel coconut bread pudding

PREP + COOK TIME **1 HOUR + STANDING** | SERVES **6**

This humble bread pudding is incredibly satisfying, easy to make, and tastes heavenly.
Serve warm or cooled with a drizzle of rich caramel sauce to top it all off.

1/2 cup (80g) vegan coconut palm sugar, divided

1 cup (250ml) canned coconut cream, divided

2 tbsp pure maple syrup

3 tsp cornstarch

2 tsp vanilla extract, divided

2 cups (500ml) almond milk

1/2 cup (125g) apple sauce

1 tsp ground cinnamon

1/2 tsp ground allspice

1/2 tsp ground nutmeg

1 1/2 lb (675g) whole grain bakery-style loaf of bread,
crusts removed, roughly chopped

1/3 cup (55g) golden raisins

1/2 cup (60g) pecans

1/2 cup (25g) dried coconut flakes, toasted (see tips)

1 Combine 1/3 cup (55g) of the sugar, 2/3 cup (180ml) of the coconut cream, maple syrup, cornstarch, and 1 teaspoon of the vanilla extract in a small saucepan; stir until smooth. Cook, stirring, over medium heat until the mixture boils and thickens. Remove from the heat.

2 Transfer half of the coconut caramel sauce to a large heatproof serving dish. (Refrigerate the remaining sauce for another purpose.). Gradually stir in the almond milk, apple sauce, spices, and the remaining 1 teaspoon vanilla extract.

3 Preheat the oven to 350°F (180°C). Grease a 9 x 13-inch (23 x 33cm) baking dish. Layer the bread, raisins, and pecans in the dish. Pour the milk mixture over the bread, making sure that all the bread is soaked. Allow to stand for 15 minutes.

4 Sprinkle the bread with the remaining coconut sugar. Bake the pudding for 45 to 50 minutes or until set.

5 Serve the pudding warm or cooled with the reserved caramel sauce, remaining coconut cream, and toasted coconut flakes.

TIPS

- To toast the coconut, stir continuously in a heavy-bottomed skillet over medium heat for 3 minutes or until lightly browned and toasted.
- If the reserved caramel sauce becomes a little thick on standing, stir in some extra coconut cream or almond milk, and reheat gently over low heat to return to a good consistency.

Chocolate ganache cupcakes

PREP + COOK TIME **45 MINUTES + COOLING + REFRIGERATION** | MAKES **12**

Fancify the cupcakes with colorful extras, such as beet powder or crushed pistachios, squares of vegan chocolate, or pretty edible flowers, or decorate as pictured here, using dehydrated pear and freeze-dried raspberry.

3/4 cup (180ml) soy milk

2 tsp apple cider vinegar

1/2 cup (110g) vegan sugar

1/4 cup (60ml) vegetable oil

1 tsp vanilla extract

3/4 cup plus 2 tbsp (100g) all-purpose flour

1/4 cup (25g) cocoa powder

1/2 tsp baking soda

1 tsp baking powder

1/2 tsp salt

chocolate ganache

7 oz (200g) vegan dark chocolate (70% cocoa), chopped

3/4 cup (180ml) canned coconut cream

1 tsp vanilla extract

1 tsp sea salt

1 Preheat the oven to 350°F (180°C). Line a 12-hole (1/3-cup/80ml) muffin pan with paper muffin cups.

2 Whisk together the soy milk and vinegar in a large bowl. Allow to stand for 5 minutes to curdle. Add the sugar, vegetable oil, and vanilla extract to the soy mixture; whisk until foamy.

3 In a small bowl, whisk together the dry ingredients. Add to the milk mixture in 2 batches, then whisk until almost smooth. Spoon the mixture into the muffin cups, filling each half full. Bake for 15 to 20 minutes or until a toothpick inserted into the center comes out clean; don't overbake. Transfer the cupcakes to a wire rack to cool.

4 Meanwhile, make the chocolate ganache. Put the chocolate in a medium heatproof bowl over a saucepan of simmering water. Stir until the chocolate is smooth; remove from the heat. Stir in the coconut cream, vanilla extract, and sea salt. Refrigerate, whisking every 10 minutes, for 30 minutes or until spreadable.

5 Serve the cupcakes topped with the ganache.

TIPS

- The cupcakes can be baked up to 2 days ahead; store in an airtight container at room temperature.
- You can freeze the cupcakes, without ganache, for up to 3 months.
- Decorate with dehydrated sliced pear (7 oz/200g) arranged on top of the cupcakes. Soak the pear in raspberry juice to make the cupcakes even more decadent, if you'd like.

Raw tiramisu

PREP TIME **45 MINUTES + STANDING, REFRIGERATION + FREEZING** | MAKES **6**

Vegan, sugar-free, and dairy-free, this creamy raw tiramisu is a modern take on the Italian classic. You can use espresso, cold-drip, or French-press coffee for the recipe.

You will need to start this recipe a day ahead

2 cups (300g) raw cashews

1^1/$_2$ cups (120g) dried flake coconut

^{3}/$_4$ cup (75g) hazelnut meal

^{1}/$_2$ cup (60g) almond meal

^{1}/$_4$ cup (20g) psyllium husks

^{1}/$_4$ cup (60ml) canned coconut milk

^{1}/$_4$ cup (60ml) coconut nectar

^{1}/$_2$ tsp vanilla extract

2 tbsp espresso coffee

2 tsp pure maple syrup

^{1}/$_4$ cup (25g) cacao powder, plus extra to decorate

coffee cream

^{1}/$_2$ cup (125ml) canned coconut cream

^{1}/$_4$ cup (60ml) pure maple syrup

^{1}/$_4$ cup (50g) coconut oil, melted

^{1}/$_3$ cup (80ml) espresso coffee

1 tsp pure vanilla extract

vanilla cream

^{3}/$_4$ cup (180ml) canned coconut cream

^{1}/$_4$ cup (60ml) pure maple syrup

^{1}/$_4$ cup (50g) coconut oil, melted

2 tsp vanilla extract

TIPS

- Store in a container in the fridge for up to 4 days.
- Coconut nectar is a sweet syrup similar to agave or maple syrup, which you can also use if you'd like.

1 Put the cashews in a medium bowl; cover with cold water. Allow to stand, covered, for 4 hours or overnight. Drain the cashews, then rinse under cold water; drain well. Reserve for the coffee cream and vanilla cream.

2 Lightly grease a 9 x 9-inch (23 x 23cm) cake pan; line the bottom with parchment paper.

3 To make the "cake" base, blend the dried coconut until finely ground; transfer to a large bowl. Stir in the ground nut meals and psyllium husks. Whisk together the coconut milk, coconut nectar, and vanilla extract in a small bowl. Add to the dry ingredients; mix until well combined. Press the mixture evenly over the bottom of the tin. Refrigerate for 30 minutes to firm up slightly.

4 Meanwhile, whisk together the coffee and maple syrup in a small bowl until combined. Set aside.

5 Make the coffee cream. Blend half of the reserved cashews with all the ingredients until as smooth as possible. (Use a high-powered blender if you have one, to achieve a very smooth consistency.)

6 Cut 12 (2–3-in/5–7.5cm) rounds from the nut base. Reserve and refrigerate 6 rounds. Dip 6 rounds, one at a time, into the coffee syrup. Lightly press into the bottoms of 6 (1-cup/250ml) glasses or jars. Don't worry if the base breaks up. Pour half of the coffee cream over the bases; dust with sifted cacao powder. Freeze for 15 minutes to firm up slightly.

7 To make the vanilla cream, using a high-powered blender if possible, blend the remaining cashews with all the ingredients until as smooth as possible. Pour half of the vanilla cream over the coffee cream layer; dust with sifted cacao powder. Freeze for 10 minutes to firm up slightly.

8 Repeat the layering with the reserved rounds dipped in coffee syrup, coffee cream, cacao powder, vanilla cream, and more cacao powder, freezing between layers. Cover; refrigerate for 6 hours or until firm. Dust with a little extra sifted cacao powder before serving.

Coconut scones

PREP + COOK TIME **40 MINUTES + COOLING & REFRIGERATION** | MAKES **12**

It's hard to pass up a good, simple scone, and these don't disappoint. They are completely vegan and use vegan margarine to keep them light and fluffy. Just remember—don't overmix the dough, and stamp out (don't twist) the rounds to cut.

3½ cups (450g) all-purpose flour

2 tsp baking powder

1 tsp salt

¼ cup (40g) vegan powdered sugar

½ cup (125g) cold vegan margarine, chopped

¾ cup (180ml) canned coconut cream, plus extra for brushing on top

1 cup (125g) fresh raspberries

1 tsp lemon juice

3 tsp vegan coconut palm sugar

1 cup (280g) coconut yogurt (use Homemade Coconut Yogurt on page 21 or purchase premade)

1 Preheat the oven to 425°F (220°C). Line 2 baking sheets with parchment paper.

2 Sift the flour, baking powder, salt, and powdered sugar into a large bowl. Add the chopped margarine, then, using your hands, combine the dry ingredients with the margarine until the dough resembles small crumbs. (You can also do this in a food processor if preferred.) Add the coconut cream and continue mixing until the mixture forms a soft dough. Press the dough onto one of the lined baking sheets at a thickness of 1 inch (2.5cm). Cover with plastic wrap and refrigerate for 30 minutes.

3 Remove the dough from the refrigerator and dust with flour if it seems sticky. Cut the dough with a 2-inch (5cm) round cutter and place on the second lined baking sheet. Brush the tops of the scones with the extra 1 tablespoon coconut milk. Bake for 15 minutes or until browned and the center scones sound hollow when tapped. Leave the scones on the baking sheet for 3 minutes before transferring to a wire rack to cool.

4 Put the raspberries, lemon juice, and coconut sugar in a medium bowl. Using a fork, crush the raspberries. Refrigerate for 30 minutes. Drain the excess liquid from the raspberries.

5 Halve the cooled scones; serve topped with the coconut yogurt and the berry mixture.

TIPS

• You can use a larger cutter and make larger scones if preferred; increase the cooking time slightly.

• These scones are best made on the day of serving, but they can also be frozen in a container for up to 2 months. To thaw the scones, wrap in foil and heat in the oven at 350°F (180°C) for 10 minutes or until heated through.

Loaded hot chocolates

Rich and indulgent, these vegan-friendly hot chocolates are desserts in themselves.
What better way could there be to keep toasty on a chilly night than to snuggle into
a comfortable seat and slowly sip and savor one of these gems?

Persian chocolate

PREP + COOK TIME **15 MINUTES** | SERVES **2**

Pit and finely chop 8 medjool dates (160g). Put 1/4 cup Dutch-process cocoa powder and 1/4 teaspoon ground cardamom in a medium deep saucepan; slowly whisk in 2 1/2 cups (625ml) almond milk until well combined. Add the chopped dates; slowly bring to the boil over low heat. Using a hand-held blender, blend on low speed until smooth. Add 1 teaspoon vanilla extract and 2 teaspoons rosewater; stir until combined. (Taste the mixture and adjust the amount of rosewater, if needed, as brands vary.) Pour into 2 large mugs. Top each mug with a handful of packaged cotton candy or vegan spun sugar. Top with 2 tablespoons slivered pistachios, 1 tablespoon cacao nibs, and edible dried rose petals, if you'd like.

Salted white caramel

PREP + COOK TIME **15 MINUTES** | SERVES **2**

Sprinkle 1/3 cup (75g) vegan sugar and 1/2 teaspoon sea salt flakes over the bottom of a medium heavy-bottomed saucepan. Place the pan over medium-low heat; cook without stirring until the sugar dissolves and forms a golden caramel. Immediately add 2 tbsp (20g) coconut oil and 1/2 cup (125ml) coconut cream; stir until the caramel melts. Remove from the heat; remove 1/4 cup (60ml) of the caramel mixture. Gradually stir 2 cups (500ml) almond milk and 2 teaspoons cornstarch into the remaining caramel mixture in the pan; cook, stirring, until the mixture boils and thickens slightly. Pour into 2 large mugs. Top with a dollop of whipped coconut cream and the reserved caramel. Scatter with caramel popcorn, if desired.

Spiced and spiked chocolate

PREP + COOK TIME **20 MINUTES + COOLING** | SERVES **2**

Put 1/2 cup (125ml) water; 1/4 orange, peeled and sliced; 2 whole star anise; 1/4 cup (60g) firmly packed vegan brown sugar; and 1/3 cup (80ml) spiced rum in a small saucepan; simmer gently over low heat until syrupy. Remove the star anise and orange slices; discard. Stir in 5 1/4 oz (150g) finely chopped vegan dark chocolate until melted and smooth. Stir in 2 cups (500ml) almond milk; bring to a simmer, stirring occasionally. Pour into 2 large mugs. Top with a generous scoop of dairy-free vanilla ice cream; dust with cocoa powder, and sprinkle with finely grated orange zest.

Thick Spanish-style chocolate

PREP + COOK TIME **15 MINUTES** | SERVES **2**

Pour 2 1/2 cups (625ml) almond milk into a medium saucepan with 2 cinnamon sticks. Remove 2 tablespoons milk from the pan; stir together with 3 teaspoons cornstarch in a small cup to a smooth paste. Slowly bring the milk almost to a boil over low heat so that the milk has time to absorb the cinnamon flavor. Add 5 1/4 oz (150g) finely chopped vegan dark chocolate, the cornstarch mixture, and a pinch of chili powder; whisk until the chocolate melts and the mixture boils and thickens slightly. Discard the cinnamon. Pour into 2 large mugs. Top with extra grated vegan dark chocolate and dust with cocoa and a pinch of cinnamon or smoked paprika.

Conversion chart

A note on measures

- One measuring cup holds approximately 8 fl oz or 250ml.

- One tablespoon holds 15ml.

- One teaspoon holds 5ml.

- The difference between one country's measuring cups and another's is within a two- or three-teaspoon variance and should not affect your cooking results.

Using measures in this book

- All cup and spoon measurements are level.

- The most accurate way of measuring dry ingredients is to weigh them.

- When measuring liquids, use a clear glass or plastic cup with measurement markings.

- All fruit and vegetables are assumed to be medium unless otherwise stated.

Dry measures

imperial	metric
$^1/_2$ oz	15g
1 oz	30g
2 oz	60g
3 oz	90g
4 oz ($^1/_4$ lb)	125g
5 oz	140g
6 oz	170g
7 oz	200g
8 oz ($^1/_2$ lb)	225g
9 oz	250g
10 oz	280g
11 oz	310g
12 oz ($^3/_4$ lb)	350g
13 oz	370g
14 oz	400g
15 oz	425g
16 oz (1 lb)	450g
24 oz ($1^1/_2$ lb)	680g
32 oz (2 lb)	900g

Liquid measures

imperial	metric
1 fl oz	30ml
2 fl oz	60ml
3 fl oz	100ml
4 fl oz	125ml
5 fl oz	150ml
6 fl oz	180ml
8 fl oz	250ml
10 fl oz	300ml
16 fl oz	500ml
20 fl oz	600ml
32 fl oz (1 qt)	1 liter

Length measures

imperial	metric
$^1/_8$ in	3mm
$^1/_4$ in	0.5cm
$^1/_2$ in	1.25cm
$^3/_4$ in	2cm
1 in	2.5cm
2 in	5cm
3 in	7.5cm
4 in	10cm
5 in	13cm
6 in	15cm
7 in	18cm
8 in	20cm
9 in	23cm
10 in	25cm
11 in	28cm
12 in (1 ft)	30cm
13 in	33cm

Oven temperatures

The oven temperatures in this book are for conventional ovens.

°F (Fahrenheit)	°C (Celsius)
250	120
300	150
325	160
350	180
375	190
400	200
425	220

Index

A

almonds
almond milk and mango pikelets 46
arugula and almond pesto 84
beet monster munch balls 56
ginger, coconut, and almond bars 168
popcorn rocky road bark 157

apples
mint apple raita 75

arancini, broccoli with arugula and almond pesto 84

arugula and almond pesto 84

arugula and walnut pesto 26

avocado
avocado and lime soft serve 162
avocado toast with smoky chickpeas 40
pea and edamame toast with avocado and umeboshi 34
rainbow avocado bowl 102
spicy black bean and avocado nachos 125

B

baked oatmeal with stone fruit 31

bananas
banana and raspberry soft serve 162
chocolate pancakes with maple banana 13
make-and-go bircher 22
spiced banana bread 148

banh mi rolls, tofu 55

bao buns, pulled jackfruit 111

beans
chickpea pancakes with spicy pinto beans 32
spiced white bean and Greek salad pitas 78
spicy black bean and avocado nachos 125
sweet potato and black bean roll ups 53

beet
beet and caraway chutney 136
beet and za'atar dip with pita chips 76
beet monster munch balls 56
beet Wellington 94

bento box 60

berries
banana and raspberry soft serve 162

berry basket cream tarts 172
blueberry coconut bars 151
buckini and berry granola clusters 28
coconut and strawberry "panna cotta" 167
crunch bowl with berry coconut yogurt 25
frozen no-bake blueberry meringue slab pie 158
make-and-go bircher 22
strawberries-and-cream "cheesecake" 152
strawberry mylkshake popsicles 154

bircher muesli
coconut tropical bircher 22
make-and-go bircher 22
pomegranate and pear bircher 22
super seed bircher 22

blueberries
blueberry coconut bars 151
frozen no-bake blueberry meringue slab pie 158
make-and-go bircher 22

bowls
miso cashew bowl 102
mixed-grain bowl 102
rainbow avocado bowl 102
spicy soba noodle bowl 102

bread
caramel coconut bread pudding 179
spiced banana bread 148

breakfast
almond milk and mango pikelets 46
avocado toast with smoky chickpeas 40
baked oatmeal with stone fruit 31
buckini and berry granola clusters 28
cherry tomato and "mozzarella" bruschetta 26
chickpea pancakes with spicy pinto beans 32
chocolate pancakes with maple banana 13
coconut tropical bircher 22
crunch bowl with berry coconut yogurt 25
crushed pea and pickled vegetable toast 44
fig and orange chia pudding 16
homemade coconut yogurt 21
make-and-go bircher 22
maple butternut waffles with pecans 43
pea and edamame toast with avocado and umeboshi 34
peanut butter and maple syrup crunch 37

pomegranate and pear bircher 22
spiced pecan French toast 14
spinach and tomato "omelet" 38
super seed bircher 22
turmeric tofu scramble 11

broccoli arancini with arugula and almond pesto 84

brownies
fudgy sweet potato brownies with espresso sauce 176
giant brownie sundae 161

bruschetta, cherry tomato and "mozzarella" 26

buckini and berry granola clusters 28

burger, the botanist 132

butter, nut and seed 18

butternut squash
maple butternut waffles with pecans 43
satay tofu and roast butternut squash wraps 81

C

cakes
chocolate ganache cupcakes 181
citrus poppyseed celebration cake 146

caramel
caramel coconut bread pudding 179
salted white caramel 186

caraway
beet and caraway chutney 136

carrot and millet patties with sunflower slaw 96

cashews
cashew pesto 112
miso cashew bowl 102
"mozzarella," vegan 26

cauliflower
cauliflower dip with rice crackers 50
masala cauliflower 128
popcorn cauliflower with spicy tomato sauce 123

Tuscan kale and lentil salad with tempeh chips 72

chard
daily greens skillet phyllo pie 135

"cheesecake," strawberries-and-cream 152

chia
fig and orange chia pudding 16

chickpeas
avocado toast with smoky chickpeas 40
the botanist burger 132
chickpea pancakes with spicy pinto
    beans 32
spinach and tomato "omelet" 38

chips
bliss and chips with smashed peas 109
tempeh chips 72

chocolate
blueberry coconut bars 151
chocolate ganache 181
chocolate ganache cupcakes 181
chocolate pancakes with maple banana 13
chocolate sauce 161
giant brownie sundae 161
peppermint bites 171
Persian hot chocolate 186
popcorn rocky road bark 157
spiced and spiked hot chocolate 186
thick Spanish-style hot chocolate 186

chutney
beet and caraway chutney 136
mint chutney 128

citrus poppyseed celebration cake 146

coconut
blueberry coconut bars 151
caramel coconut bread pudding 179
coconut and split pea curry 104
coconut and strawberry "panna cotta" 167
coconut scones 184
coconut, tomato, and lentil soup 114
coconut tropical bircher 22
crunch bowl with berry coconut yogurt 25
ginger, coconut, and almond bars 168
homemade coconut yogurt 21

coffee cream 182
cookies, King Kong 89
cream, pastry 172

curries
coconut and split pea curry 104
green curry noodles 68
Thai curry laksa 68

D
daily greens skillet phyllo pie 135
dashi 93

dips
beet and za'atar dip with pita chips 76
cauliflower dip with rice crackers 50
dosa, turmeric with masala cauliflower 128

dressings
miso peanut dressing 83
tamari sesame dressing 67

E
edamame
bento box 60
pea and edamame toast with avocado and
    umeboshi 34
wasabi edamame hummus pack 86

eggplant
bliss and chips with smashed peas 109
hoisin baked eggplant with steamed
    greens 141

espresso sauce 176

F
feta
chili tofu feta 78
lemon tofu feta 78
marinated vegan feta 38
sweet potato and black bean roll ups 53
tofu feta 78

fig and orange chia pudding 16
flatbread, mushroom and spinach 70

frozen sweet treats
avocado and lime soft serve 162
banana and raspberry soft serve 162
frozen no-bake blueberry meringue
    slab pie 158
mango and passion fruit soft
    serve 162
strawberry mylkshake popsicles 154

G
ginger, coconut, and almond bars 168

grains
mixed-grain bowl 102

green curry noodles 68

H–I
hoisin baked eggplant with steamed
    greens 141

J
jackfruit
pulled jackfruit bao buns 111

K
kale
kale chips 132
zucchini and kale frittatas 65

kebabs, tandoori tofu with mint yogurt sauce 118
King Kong cookies 89

L
lemons
lemon curd 164
lemon tofu feta 78
overnight jasmine tea and lemon curd
    rolls 164

lentils
coconut, tomato, and lentil soup 114
lentil loaf with maple glaze 131
shepherdless pie 142
Tuscan kale and lentil salad with tempeh
    chips 72

loaf, lentil with maple glaze 131

M
mac 'n' cheese, vegan 120

macadamias
mozzarella, vegan 26

make-and-go bircher 22

mangoes
almond milk and mango pikelets 46
mango and passion fruit soft serve 162

maple syrup
chocolate pancakes with maple banana 13
lentil loaf with maple glaze 131
maple butternut waffles with pecans 43
peanut butter and maple syrup crunch 37

marinara sauce 117
masala cauliflower 128

mayonnaise
everyday mayo 55
spicy mayonnaise 55
turmeric mayonnaise 55

meringue
frozen no-bake blueberry meringue slab pie 158
Italian meringue 158

Mexican quinoa pots 59

millet
  carrot and millet patties with sunflower
    slaw 96
mint
  mint apple raita 75
  mint chutney 128
  mint yogurt sauce 118
  peppermint bites 171
miso
  miso cashew bowl 102
  miso peanut bowl with shredded vegetables 83
  miso peanut dressing 83
  miso ramen noodles 68
mixed-grain bowl 102
mozzarella, vegan 26
muesli
  buckini and berry granola clusters 28
  coconut tropical bircher 22
  make-and-go bircher 22
  pomegranate and pear bircher 22
  super seed bircher 22
mushrooms
  mushroom and spinach flatbread 70
  mushroom congee 138
  mushroom, spinach, and walnut pasta 99
  mushroom "steak" sandwich 106
  spaghetti with mushroom "meatballs" 117

N

nachos, spicy black bean and avocado 125
noodles
  green curry noodles 68
  miso ramen noodles 68
  spicy not-kotsu ramen 93
  spicy soba noodle bowl 102
  sweet and spicy tofu noodles 101
  tamari noodle jars 67
  Thai curry laksa 68
  tofu tom yum noodles 68
  zucchini noodles with cashew pesto 112
nuts
  miso cashew bowl 102
  mozzarella, vegan 26
  nut and seed butter 18
  peanut butter and maple syrup crunch 37
  spiced pecan French toast 14

O

oatmeal, baked with stone fruit 31
"omelet"
  spinach and tomato "omelet" 38
oranges
  fig and orange chia pudding 16

P

pancakes
  almond milk and mango pikelets 46
  chickpea pancakes with spicy pinto beans 32
  chocolate pancakes with maple banana 13
  pancake batter 13
Parmesan, vegan 112
passion fruit
  mango and passion fruit soft serve 162
pasta
  mushroom, spinach, and walnut pasta 99
  spaghetti with mushroom "meatballs" 117
  vegan mac 'n' cheese 120
pastry cream 172
peaches
  baked oatmeal with stone fruit 31
peanuts
  miso peanut bowl with shredded vegetables 83
  miso peanut dressing 83
  peanut butter and maple syrup crunch 37
pears
  pomegranate and pear bircher 22
peas
  coconut and split pea curry 104
  crushed pea and pickled vegetable
    toast 44
  pea and edamame toast with avocado and
    umeboshi 34
  samosa wraps 62
  smashed peas 109
  sweet potato and pea samosas 75
pecans
  maple butternut waffles with pecans 43
  spiced pecan French toast 14
peppermint bites 171
Persian hot chocolate 186
pesto
  arugula and almond pesto 84
  arugula and walnut pesto 26
  cashew pesto 112

pies
  daily greens skillet phyllo pie 135
  shepherdless pie 142
pita
  beet and za'atar dip with pita chips 76
  spiced white bean and Greek salad
    pitas 78
plums
  baked oatmeal with stone fruit 31
  poached rhubarb and plums 174
polenta topping 142
pomegranate and pear bircher 22
popcorn rocky road bark 157
popsicles, strawberry mylkshake 154
potatoes
  potato bake with thyme 126
  samosa wraps 62
puddings
  caramel coconut bread pudding 179
  fig and orange chia pudding 16
  rice pudding with poached rhubarb and
    plums 174
pulled jackfruit bao buns 111

Q

quinoa
  Mexican quinoa pots 59

R

rainbow chard
  daily greens skillet phyllo pie 135
raita, mint apple 75
raspberry
  banana and raspberry soft serve 162
rhubarb
  baked oatmeal with stone fruit 31
  poached rhubarb and plums 174
rice
  bento box 60
  mushroom congee 138
  rice crackers 50
  rice pudding with poached rhubarb and
    plums 174
rolls
  overnight jasmine tea and lemon curd 164
  tofu banh mi rolls 55
roll ups, sweet potato and black bean 53

S

salads
sunflower slaw 96
Tuscan kale and lentil, with tempeh chips 72
samosas
samosa wraps 62
sweet potato and pea samosas 75
sandwich, mushroom "steak" 106
satay tofu and roast butternut squash wraps 81
sauces
beet and caraway chutney 136
chocolate sauce 161
espresso sauce 176
everyday mayo 55
marinara sauce 117
mint chutney 128
mint yogurt sauce 118
spicy mayonnaise 55
spicy tomato sauce 123
tartar sauce 109
turmeric mayonnaise 55
scones, coconut 184
seeds
nut and seed butter 18
peanut butter and maple syrup crunch 37
sunflower slaw 96
super seed bircher 22
sesame crisps 86
soft serves
avocado and lime soft serve 162
banana and raspberry soft serve 162
mango and passion fruit soft serve 162
soups
coconut, tomato, and lentil soup 114
Thai curry laksa 68
spaghetti with mushroom "meatballs" 117
spiced pecan French toast 14
spinach
mushroom and spinach flatbread 70
mushroom, spinach, and walnut pasta 99
spinach and tomato "omelet" 38
strawberries
coconut and strawberry "panna cotta" 167
strawberries-and-cream "cheesecake" 152
strawberry mylkshake popsicles 154
sunflower slaw 96
sweet and spicy tofu noodles 101

sweet potato
fudgy sweet potato brownies with espresso sauce 176
sweet potato and pea samosas 75
sweet potato and black bean roll ups 53
sunflower slaw 96

T–U

tamari
tamari noodle jars 67
tamari sesame dressing 67
tandoori tofu kebabs with mint yogurt sauce 118
tartar sauce 109
tarts, berry basket cream 172
tempeh
tempeh "bacon" bits 120
tempeh chips 72
tiramisu, raw 182
toasts
avocado toast with smoky chickpeas 40
crushed pea and pickled vegetable toast 44
pea and edamame toast with avocado and umeboshi 34
spiced pecan French toast 14
tofu
chili tofu feta 78
lemon tofu feta 78
satay tofu and roast butternut squash wraps 81
spicy not-kotsu ramen 93
sweet and spicy tofu noodles 101
tandoori tofu kebabs with mint yogurt sauce 118
tofu banh mi rolls 55
tofu feta 78
tofu tom yum noodles 68
turmeric tofu scramble 11
tomatoes
cherry tomato and "mozzarella" bruschetta 26
coconut, tomato, and lentil soup 114
marinara sauce 117
spicy tomato sauce 123
spinach and tomato "omelet" 38
turmeric
turmeric dosa with masala cauliflower 128
turmeric mayonnaise 55
turmeric tofu scramble 11

V

vanilla cream 182
vegetables
quick pickled vegetables 86
veggie patties with beet and caraway chutney 136

W–X

waffles
maple butternut waffles with pecans 43
wasabi edamame hummus pack 86
Wellington, beet 94
wraps
samosa 62
satay tofu and roast butternut squash 81

Y

yogurt
crunch bowl with berry coconut yogurt 25
homemade coconut yogurt 21
mint yogurt sauce 118

Z

za'atar
beet and za'atar dip with pita chips 76
zucchini
zucchini and kale frittatas 65
zucchini noodles with cashew pesto 112

Acknowledgments

DK would like to thank Sophia Young, Joe Reville, Amanda Chebatte, and Georgia Moore for their assistance in making this book.

The Australian Women's Weekly Test Kitchen in Sydney has developed, tested, and photographed the recipes in this book.